AAT

DEVOLVED ASSESSMENT KIT

Intermediate Units 4 and 5

Financial Records and

Cost Information

May 1998 first edition

This new Devolved Assessment Kit for *Units 4 and 5 Financial Records and Cost Information* follows the revised Intermediate Standards of Competence which are assessable from 1 June 1998. It contains:

- The **revised Standards in full**, including guidance from the AAT on **evidence requirements, sources of evidence and assessment strategy**
- The **AAT's Sample Simulation** for each Unit
- Four other **Practice Devolved Assessments** for each Unit to bring you up to speed on certain areas of the Standards
- One **Trial Run Devolved Assessment** for each Unit

All Simulations and Assessments have full solutions included in this Kit.

FOR 1998 AND 1999 ASSESSMENTS

BPP Publishing
May 1998

First edition May 1998

ISBN 0 7517 6119 0

British Library Cataloguing-in-Publication Data
A catalogue record for this book
is available from the British Library

Published by

BPP Publishing Limited
Aldine House, Aldine Place
London W12 8AW

http://www.bpp.co.uk

We are grateful to the Lead Body for Accounting for permission to reproduce extracts from the Standards of Competence for Accounting and to the AAT for permission to reproduce two of their simulations.

HOW TO USE THIS DEVOLVED ASSESSMENT KIT

Aims of this Devolved Assessment Kit

To provide the knowledge and practice to help you succeed in the devolved assessments for Intermediate Unit 4 *Financial Records and Accounts* and Unit 5 *Cost information.*

To pass the devolved assessments you need a thorough understanding in all areas covered by the standards of competence.

To tie in with the other components of the BPP Effective Study Package to ensure you have the best possible chance of success.

Interactive Texts

These cover all you need to know for devolved assessment for Unit 4 *Financial Records and Accounts* and Unit 5 *Cost Information.* Until you are ready to tackle assessment style questions at the end of your course, you only need to take these books to class. Icons clearly mark key areas of the texts. Numerous activities throughout the texts help you practise what you have just learnt.

Devolved Assessment Kit

When you have understood and practised the material in the Interactive Text, you will have the knowledge and experience to tackle this combined Devolved Assessment Kit for Units 4 and 5 *Financial Records* and *Cost Information.* This aims to get you through the devolved assessments, whether in the form of simulations or workplace assessments. It contains the AAT's sample simulations for Units 4 and 5 plus other simulations.

Central assessment Kit

Central Assessment Kit

As well as tackling the devolved assessments, you need to get to grips with the types of question that come up in central assessments. The Central Assessment Kit for Units 4 and 5 contains the AAT's sample Central Assessments for Unit 4 and Unit 5 plus relevant questions from the AAT's central assessments set under the previous version of the standards.

Recommended approach to this Devolved Assessment Kit

- To achieve competence in Units 4 and 5 (and all the other units), you need to be able to do **everything** specified by the standards. Study the Interactive Texts very carefully and do not skip any part of them .

- Learning is an **active** process. Do **all** the activities as you work through the Interactive Texts so you can be sure you really understand what you have read.

- After you have covered the material in the Interactive Texts, work through this **Devolved Assessment Kit**.

- Try the **Practice Devolved Assessments** for Unit 4 and for Unit 5 first. They are designed to test your competence in certain key areas of the Standards of Competence, but are not as comprehensive as the ones set by the AAT. They are a 'warm-up' exercise, to develop your studies from the level of the activities you did in the Intermediate Text to the level of full devolved assessment.

- Next do the **Trial Run Devolved assessments** for each unit. Although these are not yet fully at the level you can expect when you do a full devolved assessment, they do cover all the performance criteria of the elements indicated.

- Finally try both the AAT's **Sample Simulations,** which gives you the clearest idea of what full assessments will be like.

Remember this is a **practical** course.

- Try to relate the material to your experience in the workplace or any other work experience you may have had.

- Try to make as many links as you can to your study of the other Units at Intermediate level.

Changes to the 1998 Standards for Unit 4 (formerly Units 4 and 5)

The revised Standards for Unit 4 (assessable from 1 June 1998, with the first Central Assessment in December 1998) have become more specific as to what is required from you. It expressly includes the function and form of profit and loss accounts and balance sheets for sole traders, partnerships, manufacturing and club accounts, although you do not actually have to prepare them. It is important that you know which ledger accounts end up in which sections of the P & L and balance sheet.

It states, clearly which SSAPs are relevant, and expressly emphasises that double entry accounting is assessable (in Section A of the Central Assessment). Confidentiality of business transactions is also stressed. There is slightly more detail in the capital acquisition and disposal element (which used to be a separate Unit), namely on methods of funding and organisational implications of purchasing or disposing of fixed assets. There is rather less emphasis on incomplete records. Partnership accounts do *not* include appropriation.

Changes to the 1998 Standards for Unit 5 (formerly Unit 6)

The revised Standards for Unit 5 (assessable from 1 June 1998, with the first Central Assessment in December 1998) have become more specific as to what is required from you.

The main change is the inclusion of the element *Prepare and present standard cost reports* which was formerly Element 11.1 in Unit 11 *Preparing Information For Cost Analysis and Control*, and will involve the following.

- Presenting information in reports.

- Calculating the following variances as specifically stated in the guidance to Element 5.3.
  - Materials (price and usage)
  - Labour (wage rate and efficiency)
  - Overheads (expenditure, volume, efficiency and capacity)

- Explaining the significance and possible causes of variances.

- Calculating and reporting on control ratios of efficiency, capacity and activity (production volume).

The focus of the new Elements 5.1 and 5.2 is now upon whether or not a cost is **direct** or **indirect**. Other changes include the following.

- Process costing is no longer included in the standards.

- There is more emphasis on the understanding of cost behaviour.

- Activity based costing systems have now been expanded to include cost pools.

- Bases of allocating and apportioning overhead costs to responsible cost centres are now clearly spelt out: **direct; reciprocal allocation;** and the **step-down** method.

UNITS 4 AND 5 STANDARDS OF COMPETENCE

The structure of the Standards for Units 4 and 5

Each Unit commences with a statement of the **knowledge and understanding** which underpin competence in the Unit's elements.

The Unit of Competence is then divided into **elements of competence** describing activities which the individual should be able to perform.

Each element includes:

- a set of **performance criteria** which define what constitutes competent performance

- a **range statement** which defines the situations, contexts, methods etc in which competence should be displayed

- **evidence requirements**, which state that competence must be demonstrated consistently, over an appropriate time scale with evidence of performance being provided from the appropriate sources

- **sources of evidence**, being suggestions of ways in which you can find evidence to demonstrate that competence.

The elements of competence for Unit 4: *Financial Records and Accounts* are set out first, followed by those for Unit 5 *Cost Information*. Knowledge and understanding required for each Unit as a whole are listed first, followed by the performance criteria, range statements, evidence requirements and sources of evidence for each element of the Unit. Performance criteria are cross-referenced to chapters in the relevant Interactive Texts.

Unit 4: Maintaining financial records and preparing accounts

What is the unit about?

This unit is concerned with the **collecting and recording of information for the purpose of preparing accounts and maintaining effective records**. It involves identifying the types of information that are required, recording it, making any appropriate calculations or adjustments and maintaining the appropriate records.

The unit requires you to have responsibility for collecting all the relevant information for preparing accounts and presenting it to your supervisor in the form of a trial balance or an extended trial balance. Also required are communication responsibilities relating to handling queries, making suggestions for improvements and maintaining confidentiality.

Chapter references are to the Unit 4 Interactive Text

Knowledge and understanding

The business environment

- Types and characteristics of different assets and key issues relating to the acquisition and disposal of capital assets (Element 4.1)

- Relevant legislation and regulations (Elements 4.1, 4.2, 4.3 & 4.4)

- Main requirements of relevant SSAPs (Elements 4.1, 4.2, 4.3 & 4.4)

- Methods of recording information for the organisational accounts of: sole traders; partnerships; manufacturing accounts; club accounts (Element 4.2)

- Understanding the structure of the organisational accounts of: sole traders; partnerships; manufacturing accounts; club accounts (Element 4.2)

- The need to present accounts in the correct form (Element 4.3)

- The importance of maintaining the confidentiality of business transactions (Elements 4.1, 4.2, 4.3 & 4.4)

Accounting techniques

- Methods of depreciation: straight line; reducing balance (Element 4.1)

- Accounting treatment of capital items sold, scrapped or otherwise retired from service (Element 4.1)

- Use of plant registers and similar subsidiary records (Element 4.1)

- Use of transfer journal (Elements 4.1, 4.2, 4.3 & 4.4)

- Methods of funding: part exchange deals (Element 4.1)

- Accounting treatment of accruals and prepayments (Elements 4.2, 4.3 & 4.4)

- Methods of analysing income and expenditure (Element 4.2)

- Methods of restructuring accounts from incomplete evidence (Element 4.3)

- Identification and correction of different types of error (Elements 4.3 & 4.4)

- Making and adjusting provisions (Elements 4.3 & 4.4)

Accounting principles and theory

- Basic accounting concepts and principles - matching of income and expenditure within an accounting period, historic cost, accruals, consistency, prudence, materiality (Elements 4.1, 4.2, 4.3 & 4.4)

- Principles of double entry accounting (Elements 4.1, 4.2, 4.3 & 4.4)

- Distinction between capital and revenue expenditure, what constitutes capital expenditure (Element 4.1)

- Function and form of accounts for income and expenditure (Element 4.2)

- Function and form of a trial balance, profit and loss account and balance sheet for sole traders, partnerships, manufacturing accounts and club accounts (Elements 4.3 & 4.4)

- Basic principles of stock valuation: cost or NRV; what is included in cost (Elements 4.3 & 4.4)

- Objectives of making provisions for depreciation and other purposes (Elements 4.3 & 4.4)

- Function and form of final accounts (Element 4.4)

The organisation

- Understanding of the ways the accounting systems of an organisation are affected by its organisational structure, its administrative systems and procedures and the nature of its business transactions (Elements 4.1, 4.2, 4.3 & 4.4)

Element 4.1 Maintain records relating to capital acquisition and disposal

		Chapters in the Text
Performance criteria		
1	Relevant details relating to capital expenditure are correctly entered in the appropriate records	5
2	The organisation's records agree with the physical presence of capital items	5
3	All acquisition and disposal costs and revenues are correctly identified and recorded in the appropriate records	5
4	Depreciation charges and other necessary entries and adjustments are correctly calculated and recorded in the appropriate records	5
5	The records clearly show the prior authority for capital expenditure and disposal and indicate the approved method of funding and disposal	5
6	Profit and loss on disposal is correctly calculated and recorded in the appropriate records	5
7	The organisation's policies and procedures relating to the maintenance of capital records are adhered to	5
8	Lack of agreement between physical items and records are identified and either resolved or referred to the appropriate person	5
9	When possible, suggestions for improvements in the way the organisation maintains its capital records are made to the appropriate person	5
Range statement		
1	Methods of calculating depreciation: straight line; reducing balance	5
2	Records: asset register; ledger	5

Evidence requirements

- Competence must be demonstrated consistently, over an appropriate timescale with evidence of performance being provided of records being maintained.

Sources of evidence

(These are examples of sources of evidence, but candidates and assessors may be able to identify other, appropriate sources.)

- *Observed performance*, eg maintaining records of capital acquisition and disposal; calculating adjustments; calculating profit and loss on disposal; resolving discrepancies, unusual features or queries; making suggestions for improvements in the maintenance of capital records and accounts.

- *Work produced by the candidate,* eg a fixed asset register; a completed fixed asset reconciliation; a ledger; journals; invoices; minutes from meetings; cash books; disposals account or equivalent; correspondence relating to capital acquisition or disposal; authorisation for expenditure.

- *Authenticated testimonies from relevant witnesses*

- *Personal accounts of competence,* eg report of performance.

- *Other sources of evidence to prove competence of knowledge and understanding where it is not apparent from performance,* eg reports and working papers; performance in independent assessment; performance in simulation; responses to verbal questioning.

Element 4.2 Record income and expenditure

Performance criteria	Chapters in the Text
1 All income and expenditure is correctly identified and recorded in the appropriate records	2
2 Relevant accrued and prepaid income and expenditure is correctly identified and adjustments are made	8
3 The organisation's policies, regulations, procedures and timescales in relation to recording income and expenditure are observed	2
4 Incomplete data is identified and either resolved or referred to the appropriate person	10

Range statement

1 Records: day book; journal; ledger	1, 2, 7

Evidence requirements

- Competence must be demonstrated consistently, over an appropriate timescale with evidence of performance being provided from involvement with account records.

Sources of evidence

(These are examples of sources of evidence, but candidates and assessors may be able to identify other, appropriate sources.)

- *Observed performance,* eg recording income and expenditure; checking accounts; making adjustments; resolving incomplete data.

- *Work produced by the candidate,* eg nominal ledger listing; accruals and prepayments listings; petty cash book; journals for accruals and prepayments (reversibles) (recurring); invoices; minutes from meetings concerning incomplete data; cash books; disposals account or equivalent; correspondence relating to income and expenditure.

- *Authenticated testimonies from relevant witnesses.*

- *Personal accounts of competence,* eg report of performance.

- *Other sources of evidence to prove competence of knowledge and understanding where it is not apparent from performance,* eg reports and working papers; performance in independent assessment; performance in simulation; responses to verbal questioning.

Element 4.3 Collect and collate information for the preparation of final accounts

	Performance criteria	**Chapters in the Text**
1	Relevant accounts and reconciliations are correctly prepared to allow the preparation of final accounts	7
2	All relevant information is correctly identified and recorded	6
3	Investigations into business transactions are conducted with tact and courtesy	6
4	The organisation's policies, regulations, procedures and timescales relating to preparing final accounts are observed	6
5	Discrepancies and unusual features are identified and either resolved or referred to the appropriate person	10
6	The trial balance is accurately prepared and, where necessary, a suspense account is opened and reconciled	2, 7

Range statement

1	Sources of information: ledger; bank reconciliation; creditors' reconciliation; debtors' reconciliation	6, 7
2	Discrepancies and unusual features: insufficient data has been provided; inconsistencies within the data	10

Evidence requirements

- Competence must be demonstrated consistently with evidence of performance being provided of collecting and collating information for sets of final accounts from different types of organisation.

Sources of evidence

(These are examples of sources of evidence, but candidates and assessors may be able to identify other, appropriate sources.)

- *Observed performance,* eg preparing accounts and reconciliations; investigating client's business transactions; preparing the trial balance; opening and reconciling a suspense account; resolving discrepancies or unusual features.

- *Work produced by the candidate,* eg control accounts/adjusted control accounts; bank reconciliations; trial balance; audit trail; suspense account; minutes from meetings; general ledger printout; copy of the extended trial balance; nominal ledger listing; correspondence relating to income and expenditure.

- *Authenticated testimonies from relevant witnesses.*

- *Personal accounts of competence,* eg report of performance.

- *Other sources of evidence to prove competence of knowledge and understanding where it is not apparent from performance,* eg reports and working papers; performance in independent assessment; performance in simulation; responses to verbal questioning.

Element 4.4 Prepare the extended trial balance

Performance criteria	Chapters in the Text
1 Totals from the general ledger or other records are correctly entered on the extended trial balance	12
2 Material errors disclosed by the trial balance are identified, traced and referred to the appropriate authority	12
3 Adjustments not dealt with in the ledger accounts are correctly entered on the extended trial balance	12
4 An agreed valuation of closing stock is correctly entered on the extended trial balance	9, 12
5 The organisation's policies, regulations, procedures and timescales in relation to preparing extended trial balances are observed	12
6 Discrepancies, unusual features or queries are identified and either resolved or referred to the appropriate person	12
7 The extended trial balance is accurately extended and totalled	12

Range statement

1 Adjustments relating to: accruals; prepayments	12

Evidence requirements

- Competence must be demonstrated consistently, over an appropriate timescale with evidence of performance being provided from preparing an extended trial balance across the range.

Sources of evidence

(These are examples of sources of evidence, but candidates and assessors may be able to identify other, appropriate sources.)

- *Observed performance,* eg entering totals and adjustments on the extended trial balance; tracing and correcting material errors; resolving discrepancies, unusual features or queries; extending and totalling the trial balance.

- *Work produced by the candidate,* eg extended trial balance; ledger accounts; transfer journal.

- *Authenticated testimonies from relevant witnesses.*

- *Personal accounts of competence,* eg report of performance.

- *Other sources of evidence to prove competence of knowledge and understanding where it is not apparent from performance,* eg reports and working papers; performance in independent assessment; performance in simulation; responses to verbal questioning.

Unit 5:   Recording Cost Information

What is the unit about?

This unit is concerned **with recording, analysing and reporting information relating to both direct and indirect costs**. It involves the identification, coding and analysis of all costs, the apportionment and absorption of indirect costs and the presentation of all the information in standard cost reports. You are required to carry out variance analyses, different methods of allocation, apportionment and absorption and adjustments for under/over recovered indirect costs. There is also a requirement for information to be systematically checked and any unusual or unexpected results to be communicated to management.

Chapter references are to the Unit 5 Interactive Text.

The business environment

- Main types of materials: raw materials; part finished goods; materials issued from stores within the organisation; deliveries (Elements 5.1 & 5.2)

- Methods of payment for labour: salaried labour; performance related pay; profit related pay (Elements 5.1 & 5.2)

- Main types of expenses: expenses directly charged to cost units; indirect expenses; depreciation charges (Elements 5.1 & 5.2)

Accounting techniques

- Basic analysis of variances: usage; price; rate; efficiency; expenditure; volume; capacity (Elements 5.1, 5.2 & 5.3)

- Procedures for establishing standard materials costs, use of technical and purchasing information (Element 5.1)

- Methods of analysing materials usage: reasons for wastage (Element 5.1)

- Procedures for establishing standard labour costs: use of information about labour rates (Element 5.1)

- Analysis of labour rate and efficiency: idle time; overtime levels; absenteeism; sickness rates (Element 5.1)

- Methods of stock control (Element 5.1)

- Methods of setting standards for expenses (Elements 5.1 & 5.2)

- Procedures and documentation relating to expenses (Elements 5.1 & 5.2)

- Allocation of expenses to cost centres (Elements 5.1 & 5.2)

- Analysis of the effect of changing activity levels on unit costs (Elements 5.1 & 5.2)

- Procedures for establishing standard absorption rates (Element 5.2)

- Bases of allocating and apportioning indirect costs to responsibility centres: direct; reciprocal allocation; step down method (Element 5.2)

- Activity based systems of allocating costs: cost drivers; cost pools (Element 5.2)

- Bases of absorption (Element 5.2)

- Methods of presenting information orally and in written reports (Element 5.3)

- Control ratios of efficiency, capacity and activity (Element 5.3)

Accounting principles and theory

- Relationship between technical systems and costing systems - job, batch, unit, systems (Elements 5.1 & 5.2)

- Principles and objectives of standard costing systems: variance reports (Elements 5.1, 5.2 & 5.3)

- Relationships between the materials costing system and the stock control system (Element 5.1)

- Relationships between the labour costing system and the payroll accounting system (Element 5.1)

- Relationships between the expenses costing system and the accounting system (Elements 5.1 & 5.2)

- Objectives of depreciation accounting (Elements 5.1 & 5.2)

- The distinction between fixed, semi-fixed and variable costs (Elements 5.1 & 5.2)

- Effect of changes in capacity levels (Element 5.2)

- Arbitrary nature of overhead apportionments (Element 5.2)

- The significance of and possible reasons for variances (Elements 5.1, 5.2 & 5.3)

The organisation

- Understanding of the ways the accounting systems of an organisation are affected by its organisational structure, its administrative systems and procedures and the nature of its business transactions (Elements 5.1, 5.2 & 5.3)

- The reporting cycle of the organisation (Element 5.3)

Element 5.1 Record and analyse information relating to direct costs

Performance criteria		Chapters in the Text
1	Direct costs are identified in accordance with the organisation's costing procedures	2-4,9
2	Information relating to direct costs is clearly and correctly coded, analysed and recorded	2-4, 7-9
3	Direct costs are calculated in accordance with the organisation's policies and procedures	2-4, 9
4	Standard costs are compared against actual costs and any variances are analysed	10, 11
5	Information is systematically checked against the overall usage and stock control practices	10, 11
6	Queries are either resolved or referred to the appropriate person	2-4, 7

Range statement

1 Direct costs: standard and actual material costs; standard and actual labour costs; standard and actual expenses

- Materials: raw materials; part finished goods; materials issued from stores within the organisation; deliveries

- Labour: employees of the organisation on the payroll; sub-contractors; agency staff

- Expenses: direct revenue expenditure

2 Variance analysis: Materials variances: usage, price; Labour variances: rate, efficiency

Evidence requirements

- Competence must be demonstrated consistently, over an appropriate timescale with evidence of performance being provided in the recording of direct costs relating to labour, materials and expenses.

Sources of evidence

(These are examples of sources of evidence, but candidates and assessors may be able to identify other, appropriate sources.)

- *Observed performance,* eg coding information; analysing information; recording information; calculating costs; checking information against the overall usage and stock control practices; resolving queries; establishing a system for coding and analysis.

- *Work produced by the candidate,* eg records of costs; documentation relating to labour costs, materials costs and expenses; an analysis of cost information; correspondence relating to direct costs; reconciliation back to stock take.

- *Authenticated testimonies from relevant witnesses.*

- *Personal accounts of competence,* eg report of performance.

- *Other sources of evidence to prove competence of knowledge and understanding where it is not apparent from performance,* eg reports and working papers; performance in independent assessment; performance in simulation; responses to verbal questioning.

Element 5.2 Record and analyse information relating to the allocation, apportionment and absorption of overhead costs

Performance criteria	Chapters in the Text

	Performance criteria	Chapters in the Text
1	Data are correctly coded, analysed and recorded	2-4, 7
2	Overhead costs are established in accordance with the organisation's procedures	2-4, 9
3	Information relating to overhead costs is accurately and clearly recorded	2-4, 7-9
4	Overhead costs are correctly attributed to producing and service cost centres in accordance with agreed methods of allocation, apportionment and absorption	5
5	Adjustments for under or over recovered overhead costs are made in accordance with established procedures	5
6	Standard costs are compared against actual costs and any variances are analysed	10
7	Methods of allocation, apportionment and absorption are reviewed at regular intervals in discussions with senior staff, and agreed changes to methods are implemented	5
8	Staff working in operational departments are consulted to resolve any queries in the data	2-4, 7

Range statement

1   Overhead costs: standard and actual indirect material costs; standard and actual indirect labour costs; indirect expenses; depreciation charges

2   Methods of allocation and apportionment: direct; reciprocal allocation; step down method

3   Variance analysis: Overhead variances: expenditure, efficiency, volume, capacity; Fixed overhead variances: expenditure, volume, capacity, efficiency

Evidence requirements

●   Competence must be demonstrated consistently, over an appropriate timescale with evidence of performance being provided in the recording and analysis of the allocation, apportionment and absorption of indirect costs.

Sources of evidence

(These are examples of sources of evidence, but candidates and assessors may be able to identify other, appropriate sources.)

●   *Observed performance,* eg coding data; analysing data; recording data; establishing a system for coding and analysis; making adjustments for under/over recovered indirect costs; reviewing methods of allocation, apportionment and absorption; implementing changes to methods of allocation, apportionment and absorption; consulting with operational department staff.

●   *Work produced by the candidate,* eg records of costs; an analysis of cost information; correspondence relating to indirect costs; apportionment table; schedule showing over/under absorption; overhead control account.

●   *Authenticated testimonies from relevant witnesses.*

●   *Personal accounts of competence,* eg report of performance.

- Other sources of evidence to prove competence of knowledge and understanding where it is not apparent from performance, eg reports and working papers; performance in independent assessment; performance in simulation; responses to verbal questioning

Element 5.3 Prepare and present standard cost reports

Performance criteria	Chapters in the Text
1 Standard cost reports with variances clearly identified are presented in an intelligible form	11
2 Unusual or unexpected results are identified and reported to managers	11
3 Any reasons for significant variances from standard are identified and the explanations presented to management	11
4 The results of the analysis and explanations of specific variances are produced for management	11
5 Staff working in operational departments are consulted to resolve any queries in the data	11

Range statement

1   Methods of presentation: written report containing analysis and explanation of specific variances; further explanations to managers

2   Types of variances: Overhead variances: expenditure, efficiency, volume, capacity; Materials variances: usage, price; Labour variances: rate, efficiency

Evidence requirements

- Competence must be demonstrated consistently, over an appropriate timescale with evidence of performance being provided from both methods of presentation.

Sources of evidence

(These are examples of sources of evidence, but candidates and assessors may be able to identify other, appropriate sources.)

- Observed performance, eg presenting standard cost reports; reporting unusual or unexpected results to managers; presenting explanations for significant variances from standard to management; analysing specific variances; consulting with staff.

- Work produced by the candidate, eg section of the cost reporting cycle; written report of specific variances; correspondence with management.

- Authenticated testimonies from relevant witnesses.

- Personal accounts of competence, eg report of performance.

- Other sources of evidence to prove competence of knowledge and understanding where it is not apparent from performance, eg reports and working papers; performance in independent assessment; performance in simulation; responses to verbal questioning.

ASSESSMENT STRATEGY

These units are assessed by two *central assessments* (3 hours each) and by *devolved* assessment.

Central Assessment *(more detail can be found in the Central Assessment Kit)*

A central assessment is a means of collecting evidence that you have the **essential knowledge and understanding** which underpins competence. It is also a means of collecting evidence across the **range of contexts** for the standards, and of your ability to **transfer skills**, knowledge and understanding to different situations. Thus, although central assessments contain practical tests linked to the performance criteria, they also focus on the underpinning knowledge and understanding. You should in addition expect each central assessment to contain tasks taken from across a broad range of the standards.

Devolved Assessment

Devolved assessment is a means of collecting evidence of your ability to carry out **practical activities** and to **operate effectively in the conditions of the workplace** to the standards required. Evidence may be collected at your place of work or at an Approved Assessment Centre by means of simulations of workplace activity, or by a combination of these methods.

If the Approved Assessment Centre is a **workplace**, you may be observed carrying out accounting activities as part of your normal work routine. You should collect documentary evidence of the work you have done, or contributed to, in an **accounting portfolio**. Evidence collected in a portfolio can be assessed in addition to observed performance or where it is not possible to assess by observation.

Where the Approved Assessment Centre is a **college or training organisation**, devolved assessment will be by means of a combination of the following.

- Documentary evidence of activities carried out at the workplace, collected by you in an **accounting portfolio.**

- Realistic **simulations** of workplace activities. These simulations may take the form of case studies and in-tray exercises and involve the use of primary documents and reference sources.

- **Projects and assignments** designed to assess the Standards of Competence.

If you are unable to provide workplace evidence you will be able to complete the assessment requirements by the alternative methods listed above.

Assessment method	Suitable for assessing
Performance of an accounting task either in the workplace or by simulation: eg preparing and processing documents, posting entries, making adjustments, balancing, calculating, analysing information etc by manual or computerised processes	**Basic task competence.** Adding supplementary oral questioning may help to draw out underpinning knowledge and understanding and highlight your ability to deal with contingencies and unexpected occurrences
General case studies. These are broader than simulations. They include more background information about the system and business environment	Ability to **analyse a system** and suggest ways of modifying it. It could take the form of a written report, with or without the addition of oral or written questions
Accounting problems/cases: eg a list of balances that require adjustments and the preparation of final accounts	Understanding of the **general principles of accounting** as applied to a particular case or topic
Preparation of flowcharts/diagrams. To illustrate an actual (or simulated) accounting procedure	**Understanding of the logic** behind a procedure, of controls, and of relationships between departments and procedures. Questions on the flow chart or diagram can provide evidence of underpinning knowledge and understanding
Interpretation of accounting information from an actual or simulated situation. The assessment could include non-financial information and written or oral questioning	**Interpretative competence**
Preparation of written reports on an actual or simulated situation	**Written communication skills**
Analysis of critical incidents, problems encountered, achievements	Your ability to handle **contingencies**
Listing of likely errors eg preparing a list of the main types of errors likely to occur in an actual or simulated procedure	Appreciation of the range of **contingencies** likely to be encountered. Oral or written questioning would be a useful supplement to the list
Outlining the organisation's policies, guidelines and regulations	Performance criteria relating to these aspects of competence. It also provides evidence of competence in **researching information**
Objective tests and short-answer questions	**Specific knowledge**
In-tray exercises	Your **task-management ability** as well as technical competence
Supervisors' reports	**General job competence**, personal effectiveness, reliability, accuracy, and time management. Reports need to be related specifically to the Standards of Competence
Analysis of work logbooks/diaries	**Personal effectiveness**, time management etc. It may usefully be supplemented with oral questioning

Assessment method	Suitable for assessing
Formal written answers to questions	Knowledge and understanding of the **general accounting environment** and its impact on particular units of competence.
Oral questioning	**Knowledge and understanding** across the range of competence including organisational procedures, methods of dealing with unusual cases, contingencies and so on. It is often used in conjunction with other methods.

Unit 4
Financial Records

SAMPLE SIMULATION

INTERMEDIATE STAGE - NVQ/SVQ3

Unit 4

Maintaining Financial Records

and Preparing Accounts

(AAT Sample)

This Sample Simulation is the AAT's Sample Simulation for Unit 4. Its purpose is to give you an idea of what an AAT simulation looks like. It is not intended as a definitive guide to the tasks you may be required to perform.

The suggested time allowance for this Assessment is four hours. Up to 30 minutes extra time may be permitted in an AAT simulation. Breaks in assessment will be allowed in the AAT simulation, but it must normally be completed in one day.

Calculators may be used but no reference material is permitted.

DO NOT OPEN THIS PAPER UNTIL YOU ARE READY TO START
UNDER TIMED CONDITIONS

INSTRUCTIONS

This Simulation is designed to test your ability to maintain financial records and prepare accounts.

The situation is provided on Page 5.

The tasks you are to perform are set out on Page 6 and 7.

You are provided with data which you must use to complete the tasks.

Your answers should be set out in the answer booklet on Pages 15 to 35 using the documents provided.

You are allowed **four hours** to complete your work.

A high level of accuracy is required. Check your work carefully.

Correcting fluid may be used in moderation. Errors should be crossed out neatly and clearly. You should write in black ink, not pencil.

You are advised to read the whole of the Simulation before commencing as all of the information may be of value and is not necessarily supplied in the sequence in which you might wish to deal with it.

A full suggested solution to this Simulation is provided in this Kit on Pages 105 to 120.

THE SITUATION

Your name is Val Denning and you are an accounts assistant working for Branson & Co, a partnership business owned by two partners called Amy Brandreth and Sanjay Sondin. You report to the firm's Accountant, Jenny Holden.

Branson is a manufacturing business, purchasing raw materials and producing a finished product called a mendip. The manufacturing process is very simple, involving the assembly of just two bought-in parts and a small amount of finishing work. The firm's stocks consist of raw materials (the bought-in parts) and finished mendips; work in progress is negligible in value at any time.

Books and records

Branson maintains a full system of ledger accounts in manual format. Money coming in and going out is recorded in a manual cash book which serves both as a book of prime entry and a ledger account.

Branson also maintains a manual fixed assets register. This includes details of capital expenditure (but not revenue expenditure) incurred in acquiring or enhancing fixed assets, as well as details of depreciation and disposals.

Accounting policies and procedures

Branson is registered for VAT and all of its sales are standard-rated.

Branson classifies its fixed assets into three categories: company cars, plant and equipment, and other fixed assets. For each category the nominal (general) ledger includes accounts relating to cost, depreciation charge (ie the profit and loss expense), accumulated depreciation (ie the balance sheet provision), and disposals.

Company cars are depreciated at a rate of 45% per annum on the reducing balance. Plant and equipment and other fixed assets are depreciated at 25% per annum straight line, assuming nil residual value. In the year of an asset's acquisition a full year's depreciation is charged, regardless of the exact date of acquisition. In the year of an asset's disposal, no depreciation is charged. Company car running costs are recorded in the firm's accounts as an administration overhead. Branson is not able to recover input VAT on the purchase of company cars. Similarly, the firm is not required to account for output VAT when company cars are disposed of.

Authorisation for the acquisition and disposal of fixed assets, and for the method of finance, derives from the partners and is communicated to you by means of a memo from the firm's Accountant at the beginning of each month in which an acquisition or disposal is planned. In the month of March 1998 one acquisition and one disposal took place; these are referred to in the memo on Page 8.

The simulation

In this simulation you will be required to perform a number of tasks leading up to the preparation of an extended trial balance for the year ended 31 March 1998.

TASKS TO BE COMPLETED

In the answer booklet on Pages 15 to 35 complete the tasks outlined below. Data for this assessment is provided on Pages 8 to 13.

1   Refer to the memo on Page 8 and the supplier's invoice on Page 9. This refers to the purchase of a new company car and the trade-in of an existing company car. Record the acquisition and the trade-in in the fixed assets register (see Pages 17-19 in the answer booklet) and in the nominal (general) ledger (see Pages 21-22 in the answer booklet). You are reminded that Branson is *not* able to recover VAT on the acquisition of company cars.

2   By reference to the fixed assets register, calculate the depreciation for the year on each of the company cars and on each item of plant and equipment. You should record the relevant amounts in the fixed assets register and in the nominal (general) ledger. You should also calculate the depreciation for the year on 'other fixed assets' by reference to the relevant account in the nominal (general) ledger and record the amount in the nominal (general) ledger.

3   A member of staff has listed the company cars actually present on Branson's premises at close of business on 31 March 1998. His list is on Page 10. Compare this list with the details recorded in the fixed assets register and describe any discrepancies in a memo to the firm's Accountant. Use the memo form on Page 30 of the answer booklet.

4   The nominal (general) ledger already includes sales and purchases transactions up to 28 February 1998. The sales and purchases day books have been totalled for March 1998 and the totals are displayed on Page 10. Post these totals to the nominal (general) ledger. Note that the invoice from Task 1 was *not* included in the March totals because it was not received until April.

5   Refer to the business bank statement and the business cash book on Pages 11 and 12. Perform a bank reconciliation as at 31 March 1998. Set out your reconciliation on Page 31 of the answer booklet.

6   Post from the business cash book to the nominal (general) ledger for the month of March 1998.

7   Bring down a balance as at 1 April 1998 on each account in the nominal (general) ledger and enter the balances in the first two columns of the trial balance (see Page 32 of the answer booklet). The totals of the two columns will not be equal. You should establish why, and make the appropriate addition to the trial balance.

8   The debit entry in the suspense account (£750) represents a cheque made out on the business bank account earlier in the year. The payee is not known to you as a supplier or employee of Branson. Describe how you would ascertain the nature of this payment so that you can account for it correctly. Set out your answer on Page 33 of the answer booklet.

   (*Note: once you have completed this task you should ask your assessor to explain what the payment represents. You will need this information to complete Task 9*).

9   The credit entry on the suspense account is the proceeds on disposal of a fixed asset included in the category 'other fixed assets'. No other entries have been made in the nominal ledger in respect of this disposal. The asset originally cost £2,317.69, and its accumulated depreciation at 31 March 1997 was £946.23. Draft journal entries, dated 31 March 1998, to clear the balance on the suspense account. Set out your entries, with full narrative, on Page 34 of the answer booklet. (Note: you are *not* required to adjust the nominal (general) ledger accounts in the light of this transaction.)

10 Details of Branson's closing stocks are given on Page 13. Calculate the value of closing stock of raw materials and finished goods at 31 March 1998 for inclusion in the trial balance. Use the blank Page 35 of the answer booklet for your answer. Note that to calculate the value of finished goods stock you will need to prepare a manufacturing account for the year ended 31 March 1998.

11 On the trial balance, make appropriate adjustments in respect of the following matters.

    (a) The journal entries prepared in Task 9

    (b) Closing stock calculated in Task 10

    (c) Accruals and prepayments. For details of these see Page 13.

12 Extend the trial balance. This includes totalling all columns of the trial balance and making entries to record the net profit or loss for the year ended 31 March 1998.

DATA

MEMO

To: Val Denning

From: Jenny Holden

Subject: Fixed asset acquisitions/disposals in March 1998

Date: 2 March 1998

Only one fixed asset acquisition is planned for the month of March. Our salesman, Andy Noble, will trade in his old car (registration M104PTY) and purchase a new one. The new one will be financed partly by the trade-in value (agreed at £1,850), and partly by cash.

<u>*SALES INVOICE*</u>

HYLEX MOTORS
BLANKTON

VAT registration: 318 1627 66

Extines Road, Blankton
Telephone: 01489 22514   Fax: 01489 56178

Date/tax point: 27 March 1998

Invoice to:

Invoice number: 42176

Branson & Co
Unit 6 Chalmers Industrial Estate
Blankton
BT3 4NY

Registration: R261 GHT   Registration date: 27/3/98   Stock number: Q4510
Chassis no: TWQQAW 66780   Engine no: ER43218   Sales person: M Easton

	£
Ford Mondeo	
List price	10,900.10
VAT at 17.5%	1,907.50
	12,807.50
Vehicle excise duty (12 months)	140.00
Total due	12,947.50
Less: part-exchange (M104 PTY)	1,850.00
Balance to pay	11,097.50

Terms: net, 30 days

Company cars on the premises, 31 March 1998

P321 HDR - in yard

N33 FGY - in yard

R261 GHT - in yard

Sales day book totals, March 1998

	£
Total value of invoices	36,514.59
Sales value	31,076.25
VAT	5,438.34

Purchases day book totals, March 1998

	£
Total value of invoices	9,133.18
Administration overheads	991.24
Factory overheads	1,451.09
Purchases	4,871.22
Selling and distribution overheads	524.87
VAT	1,294.76

Northern Bank plc

STATEMENT

26 High Street, Blankton BT1 6FG

45-32-20

Account: Branson & Co

Statement no: 192

Account no: 28771243

Details	Payments £	Receipts £	Date	Balance £
			1998	
Balance forward			1-Mar	1,912.90
19328	1,105.36		3-Mar	807.54
CC		4,227.18	4-Mar	5,034.72
19332	365.11		10-Mar	4,669.61
CC		4,265.77	11-Mar	8,935.38
19331	1,192.45		12-Mar	7,742.93
19333	2,651.08		16-Mar	5,091.85
CC		5,931.20	18-Mar	11,023.05
19335	299.52		23-Mar	10,723.53
19334	3,006.12		24-Mar	7,717,41
CC		3,773.81	25-Mar	11,491.22
19340	10,480.05		30-Mar	1,011.17
19336	2,561.29		31-Mar	1,550.12 O/D

Key S/O Standing order   DD Direct debit   CC Cash and/or cheques   CHGS Charges
BACS Bankers automated clearing services   O/D Overdrawn

CASHBOOK

RECEIPTS			PAYMENTS					CB122
			Date	Details	Cheque no			
Total £	Sales ledger control £	Other £	1998			Total £	Purchases ledger control £	Other £
5,034.72			1-Mar	Balance b/f				
4,265.77	4,265.77		6-Mar	Cash and cheques banked				
5,931.20	5,931.20		13-Mar	Cash and cheques banked				
3,773.81	3,773.81		20-Mar	Cash and cheques banked				
6,071.88	6,071.88		27-Mar	Cash and cheques banked				
5,512.67	5,512.67		31-Mar	Cash and cheques banked				
			3-Mar	Hanway plc	19331	1,192.45	1,192.45	
			5-Mar	Peters Limited	19332	365.11	365.11	
			9-Mar	Wright & Parkin	19333	2,651.08	2,651.08	
			16-Mar	Westcott Limited	19334	3,006.12	3,006.12	
			17-Mar	Sidlow & Morris	19335	299.52	299.52	
			24-Mar	Harper John & Co	19336	2,561.29	2,561.29	
			24-Mar	Paul Darby plc	19337	278.01	278.01	
			27-Mar	Brandreth: drawings	19338	500.00		500.00
			27-Mar	Sondin: drawings	19339	450.00		450.00
			27-Mar	Wages and salaries (see analysis below)	19340	10,480.05		10,480.05
			31-Mar	Balance c/d		8,806.42		
30,590.05	25,555.33					30,590.05	10,353.58	11,430.05
8,806.42			1-Apr	Balance b/d				
				Wages and salaries analysis				
				Direct labour				6,014.73
				Admin overhead				1,105.69
				Factory overhead				1,931.75
				Sell and dist overhead				1,427.88
								10,480.05

Stock at 31 March 1998

Raw materials

	Cost	Net realisable value
	£	£
Material X	3,417.22	3,817.66
Material Y	5,441.08	4,719.33

Finished mendips

A total of 25,613 units were produced in the year ended 31 March 1998, of which 3,117 units remained in stock at the year end.

Accruals and prepayments at 31 March 1998

Branson & Co do not attempt to calculate accruals and prepayments for immaterial amounts, defined as being anything less than £200.

The only two items which may amount to more than this are included in administration overheads, as follows.

- Office rental of £3,250 was paid in December 1997 in respect of the six months ending 30 June 1998.
- Telephone and fax charges amount to about £630 per quarter. At 31 March 1998 these charges had already been paid for the quarter ended 31 January 1998, but the invoice for the subsequent quarter is not expected to arrive until May 1998.

SAMPLE SIMULATION

Maintaining Financial Records and Preparing Accounts

ANSWER BOOKLET

ANSWERS (Tasks 1, 2)

EXTRACTS FROM FIXED ASSETS REGISTER

Description/serial no	Location	Date acquired	Original cost £	Enhance-ments £	Total £	Deprecia-tion £	NBV £	Funding method	Disposal proceeds £	Disposal date £
Plant and equipment										
Milling machine 45217809	Factory	20/6/94	3,456.08		3,456.08			Cash		
Year ended 31/3/95						864.02	2,592.06			
Year ended 31/3/96						864.02	1,728.04			
Year ended 31/3/97						864.02	864.02			
" " 31/3/99						864.02	—			
Lathe 299088071	Factory	12/6/95	4,008.24		4,008.24			Cash		
Year ended 31/3/96						1,002.06	3,006.18			
Year ended 31/3/97						1,002.06	2,004.12			
						1,002.06	1,002.06			
Drill assembly 51123412	Factory	12/2/96	582.44		582.44			Cash		
Year ended 31/3/96						145.61	436.83			
Year ended 31/3/97						145.61	291.22			
						145.61	145.61			
Punch drive 91775321	Factory	12/2/96	1,266.00		1,266.00			Cash plus trade-in		
Year ended 31/3/96						316.50	949.50			
Year ended 31/3/97						316.50	633.00			
						316.50	316.50			
Winding gear 53098871	Factory	13/3/96	1,082.68		1,082.68			Cash		
Year ended 31/3/96						270.67	812.01			
Year ended 31/3/97			341.79	1,153.80		384.60	769.20			
						288.45	480.75			
						384.00				

ANSWERS (Tasks 1, 2, continued)

EXTRACTS FROM FIXED ASSETS REGISTER

Description/serial no	Location	Date acquired	Original cost £	Enhance-ments £	Total £	Deprecia-tion £	NBV £	Funding method	Disposal proceeds £	Disposal date £
Tender press 44231809	Factory	8/8/96	4,256.04		4,256.04					
						1,064.01	3,192.03	Cash		
						1064 01	2128 02			

ANSWERS (Tasks 1, 2, continued)

EXTRACTS FROM FIXED ASSETS REGISTER

Description/serial no	Location	Date acquired	Original cost £	Enhancements £	Total £	Depreciation £	NBV £	Funding method	Disposal proceeds £	Disposal date £
Company cars										
M412 RTW	Yard	25/8/94	8,923.71		8,923.71			Lease		
Year ended 31/3/95						4,015.67	4,908.04			
Year ended 31/3/96						2,208.62	2,699.42			
Year ended 31/3/97						1,214.74	1,484.68			
						668.11	816.57			
M104 PTY	Yard	15/3/95	8,643.00		8,643.00			Cash	1850	27.3.98
Year ended 31/3/95						3,889.35	4,753.65			
Year ended 31/3/96						2,139.14	2,614.51			
Year ended 31/3/97						1,176.53	1,437.98			
N33 FGY	Yard	18/9/95	10,065.34		10,065.34			Cash plus trade-in		
Year ended 31/3/96						4,529.40	5,535.94			
Year ended 31/3/97						2,491.17	3,044.77			
						1370.15	1674.62			
P321 HDR	Yard	13/12/96	9,460.26		9,460.26			Cash		
Year ended 31/3/97						4,527.12	5,535.14			
R261 GHT	Yard	27/3/98	12807.50		12807.50	5,763.38	7,044.12	Cash plus trade in		
Year ended 31/3/98										

ANSWERS (Tasks 1, 2, 4, 6, 7)

NOMINAL (GENERAL) LEDGER

Account Administration overheads

Debit			Credit		
Date 1998	Details	Amount £	Date 1998	Details	Amount £
1 Mar	Balance b/f	15,071.23			

Account Brandreth capital account

Debit			Credit		
Date 1998	Details	Amount £	Date 1998	Details	Amount £
			1 Mar	Balance b/f	17,063.24

Account Administration overheads

Debit			Credit		
Date 1998	Details	Amount £	Date 1998	Details	Amount £
1 Mar	Balance b/f	11,056.73			

140 - Cae Tax

ANSWERS (Tasks 1, 2, 4, 6, 7 continued)

NOMINAL (GENERAL) LEDGER

Account Company cars: cost

Debit			Credit		
Date 1998	Details	Amount £	Date 1998	Details	Amount £
1 Mar 28 mar	Balance b/f Bank Trade in	37,092.31 1280750 1850.00	28 Mard	Disposal	8643.00

Account Company cars: depreciation charge

Debit			Credit		
Date 1998	Details	Amount £	Date 1998	Details	Amount £
31 Mar	Annual dep	983884			

Account Company cars: accumulated depreciation

Debit			Credit		
Date 1997	Details	Amount £	Date 1997	Details	Amount £
	Disposal		1 Apr	Balance b/f	25,921.74 983884 35760.58

ANSWERS (Tasks 1, 2, 4, 6, 7 continued)

NOMINAL (GENERAL) LEDGER

Account Company cars: disposals
Debit   Credit

Date 1998	Details	Amount £	Date 1998	Details	Amount £
28 March	Asset P + L	8643.00 409.02	28 March	Accum depn Trade in	7205.02 1850.00 9052.02

Account Direct labour costs
Debit   Credit

Date 1998	Details	Amount £	Date 1998	Details	Amount £
1 Mar	Balance b/f	60,012.64			

Account Factory overheads
Debit   Credit

Date 1998	Details	Amount £	Date 1998	Details	Amount £
1 Mar	Balance b/f	27,109.67			

ANSWERS (Tasks 1, 2, 4, 6, 7 continued)

NOMINAL (GENERAL) LEDGER

Account Other fixed assets: cost
Debit   Credit

Date 1998	Details	Amount £	Date 1998	Details	Amount £
1 Mar	Balance b/f	18,923.50			

Account Other fixed assets: depreciation charge
Debit   Credit

Date 1998	Details	Amount £	Date 1998	Details	Amount £

Account Other fixed assets: accumulated depreciation
Debit   Credit

Date 1997	Details	Amount £	Date 1997	Details	Amount £
			1 Apr	Balance b/f	6,224.12

ANSWERS (Tasks 1, 2, 4, 6, 7 continued)

NOMINAL (GENERAL) LEDGER

Account Other fixed assets: disposals

Debit			Credit		
Date 1998	Details	Amount £	Date 1998	Details	Amount £

Account Plant and equipment: cost

Debit			Credit		
Date 1998	Details	Amount £	Date 1998	Details	Amount £
1 Mar	Balance b/f	14,993.27			

Account Plant and equipment: depreciation charge

Debit			Credit		
Date 1998	Details	Amount £	Date 1998	Details	Amount £

ANSWERS (Tasks 1, 2, 4, 6, 7 continued)

NOMINAL (GENERAL) LEDGER

Account Plant and equipment: accumulated depreciation

Debit   Credit

Date 1997	Details	Amount £	Date 1997	Details	Amount £
			1 Apr	Balance b/f	7,239.68

Account Plant and equipment: disposals

Debit   Credit

Date 1998	Details	Amount £	Date 1998	Details	Amount £

Account Purchases

Debit   Credit

Date 1998	Details	Amount £	Date 1998	Details	Amount £
1 Mar	Balance b/f	54,231.89			

ANSWERS (Tasks 1, 2, 4, 6, 7 continued)

NOMINAL (GENERAL) LEDGER

Account Purchases ledger control

Debit			Credit		
Date 1998	Details	Amount £	Date 1998	Details	Amount £
			1 Mar	Balance b/f	18,457.20

Account Sales

Debit			Credit		
Date 1998	Details	Amount £	Date 1998	Details	Amount £
			1 Mar	Balance b/f	225,091.42

Account Sales ledger control

Debit			Credit		
Date 1998	Details	Amount £	Date 1998	Details	Amount £
1 Mar	Balance b/f	24,617.03			

ANSWERS (Tasks 1, 2, 4, 6, 7 continued)

NOMINAL (GENERAL) LEDGER

Account Selling and distribution overheads

Debit			Credit		
Date 1998	Details	Amount £	Date 1998	Details	Amount £
1 Mar	Balance b/f	14,303.02			
28 Mar	Car Tax	140,00			

Account Sondin capital account

Debit			Credit		
Date 1998	Details	Amount £	Date 1998	Details	Amount £
			1 Mar	Balance b/f	8,703.28

Account Sondin current account

Debit			Credit		
Date 1998	Details	Amount £	Date 1998	Details	Amount £
1 Mar	Balance b/f	12,912.29			

ANSWERS (Tasks 1, 2, 4, 6, 7 continued)

NOMINAL (GENERAL) LEDGER

Account Stock: raw materials

Debit			Credit		
Date 1997	Details	Amount £	Date 1998	Details	Amount £
1 Apr	Balance b/f	6,294.33			

Account Stock: finished goods

Debit			Credit		
Date 1997	Details	Amount £	Date 1998	Details	Amount £
1 Apr	Balance b/f	12,513.77			

Account Suspense

Debit			Credit		
Date 1998	Details	Amount £	Date 1998	Details	Amount £
26 Jan	Bank	750.00	24 Feb	Bank	1,124.55

ANSWERS (Tasks 1, 2, 4, 6, 7 continued)

NOMINAL (GENERAL) LEDGER

Account VAT Debit			Credit		
Date 1998	Details	Amount £	Date 1998	Details	Amount £
			1 Mar	Balance b/f	5,091.27

ANSWERS (Task 3)

MEMO
To:
From:
Subject:
Date:

ANSWERS (Task 5)

ANSWERS (Tasks 7, 11, 12)

TRIAL BALANCE AT 31 MARCH 1998

Account name	Balances per ledger		Adjustments		Profit and loss account		Balance sheet	
	£	£	£	£	£	£	£	£

ANSWERS (Tasks 8)

ANSWERS (Tasks 9)

JOURNAL

Date 1998	Account names and narrative	Debit £	Credit £

ANSWERS (Task 10)

Practice devolved assessments

Practice devolved assessment
1 *Reggie Stir*

Performance criteria

The following performance criteria are covered in this Devolved Assessment.

Element 4.1: Maintain records and accounts relating to capital acquisition and disposal

1	Relevant details relating to capital expenditure are correctly entered in the appropriate records
3	All acquisition and disposal costs and revenues are correctly identified and recorded in the appropriate records
6	Profit or loss on disposal is correctly calculated and recorded in the appropriate records
7	The organisation's policies and procedures relating to the maintenance of capital records are adhered to

Notes on completing the Assessment

This Assessment is designed to test your ability to record capital transactions in the journal, the fixed assets register and the ledger.

You are provided with data (Page 40) which you must use to complete the tasks on Page 41.

You are allowed **two hours** to complete your work.

A high level of accuracy is required. Check your work carefully.

Correcting fluid should not be used. Errors should be crossed out neatly and clearly. You should write in ink and not in pencil.

A full suggested solution to this Assessment is provided on Page 121.

Do not turn to the suggested solution until you have completed all parts of the Assessment.

PRACTICE DEVOLVED ASSESSMENT 1: REGGIE STIR

Data

Reggie Stir Ltd is a small company producing many different kinds of jugs. Skilled craftsmen make the jugs on a potter's wheel. They are then fired in a kiln and distributed by van to various gift shops.

You are Fletcher Clink, an accounting technician and your boss is Nick McKay, the financial controller. Mr McKay is concerned that the records relating to fixed assets should be kept up to date.

The company, which operates from rented premises, does not have a large number or turnover of fixed assets, the main ones being three potter's wheels, four kilns, one pugmill (a long tube for turning the clay), three delivery vans and various items of furniture, all of which were bought some time ago and are fully depreciated.

The firm keeps a manual fixed assets register, the relevant pages of which are reproduced below.

PLANT AND EQUIPMENT

Ref	Description	Date of purchase	Cost £	Depreciation period	Accumulated depreciation 31 Dec 1994 £	Date of disposal	Net book value 31 Dec 1994 £	Sale/scrap proceeds £	Loss/ profit £
1/K	Kiln	1 Jan 1993	1200	6 years	400		800		
1/P	Pugmill	1 July 1994	300	4 years	75		225		
2/K	Kiln	1 Mar 1992	600	6 years	300		300		
3/K	Kiln	20 Aug 1991	750	6 years	500		250		
1/W	Wheel	31 Mar 1993	400	4 years	200		200		
2/W	Wheel	1 Feb 1992	400	4 years	300		100		
4/K	Kiln	1 Sep 1992	900	6 years	450		450		
3/W	Wheel	1 Mar 1994	420	4 years	105		315		
Totals			4970		2330		2640		

MOTOR VEHICLES

Ref	Description	Date of purchase	Cost £	Depreciation type	Accumulated depreciation 31 Dec 1994 £	Date of disposal	Net book value 31 Dec 1994 £	Sale/scrap proceeds £	Loss/ profit £
1/V	Van reg G249 NPO	1 Feb 1990	4000	Reducing balance 25%	3051		949		
2/V	Van reg K697 JKL	1 June 1993	6000	Reducing balance 25%	2625		3375		
3/V	Van reg M894 TMG	30 Sep 1994	8000	Reducing balance 25%	2000		6000		
Totals			18000		7676		10324		

It is the firm's policy to charge a full year's depreciation in the year of purchase and none in the year of sale. Plant and equipment are depreciated on a straight line basis over the periods shown on the register. Motor vehicles are all depreciated at a rate of 25% using the reducing balance method.

During 1995 the following transactions in fixed assets took place.

(a) On 3 August an old kiln (ref. 1/K) was traded in at Cumere Oven Ltd and a new one (ref. 5/K) purchased for £1,600 from the same supplier. A trade-in allowance of £500 was given for the old kiln, the balance to be settled at a later date. An invoice (no. 35X42) was raised by the supplier for the amount in question.

(b) On 5 September, a new potter's wheel (ref. 4/W) was purchased for £500 cash.

(c) On 10 October the oldest delivery van (ref. 1/V) was traded in for a new one (ref. 4/V), registration N583 MNO, costing £9,000. The supplier, Van Guard Ltd, gave a trade-in allowance of £1,000 on the old van and raised an invoice (no. Z/2643) for the difference.

It is now 31 December 1995 and you have been asked to help prepare the year-end accounts.

Tasks

(a) Record the above transactions and the year-end provisions for depreciation in:

    (i)   the journal;
    (ii)   the ledger accounts;
    (iii) the fixed assets register.

(b) Produce an extract from the year-end balance sheet showing the following.

    (i)   Plant and equipment (cost)
    (ii)   Motor vehicles (cost)
    (iii) Plant and equipment (provision for depreciation)
    (iv) Motor vehicles (provision for depreciation)

All workings should be to the nearest £.

The relevant ledger accounts, journal pages and fixed assets register page are attached for you to complete.

Tutorial note. In practice you would post from the journal to the ledger accounts, but in this exercise you may find it helpful to do the opposite in order to calculate any profit or loss on disposal of fixed assets.

	JOURNAL			Page 50
Date	Details	Folio Ref	£	£

JOURNAL				Page 51
Date	Details	Folio Ref	£	£

LEDGER ACCOUNTS

PLANT AND EQUIPMENT

	£		£
Date		*Date*	
1995		*1995*	
1 Jan Balance b/f	4,970		

PLANT AND EQUIPMENT: PROVISION FOR DEPRECIATION

	£		£
		Date	
		1995	
		1 Jan Balance b/f	2,330

PLANT AND EQUIPMENT: DISPOSALS

	£		£

MOTOR VEHICLES

	£		£
Date			
1995			
1 Jan Balance b/f	18,000		

MOTOR VEHICLES: PROVISION FOR DEPRECIATION

	£		£
		Date	
		1995	
		1 Jan Balance b/f	7,676

MOTOR VEHICLES: DISPOSALS

	£		£

PLANT AND EQUIPMENT										
Ref	Description	Date of purchase	Cost £	Depreciation period	Accumulated depreciation 31 Dec 1995 £	Date of disposal	Net book value 31 Dec 1995 £	Sale/scrap proceeds £	Loss/ profit £
1/K	Kiln	1 Jan 1993	1200	6 years					
1/P	Pugmill	1 July 1994	300	4 years					
2/K	Kiln	1 Mar 1992	600	6 years					
3/K	Kiln	20 Aug 1991	750	6 years					
1/W	Wheel	31 Mar 1993	400	4 years					
2/W	Wheel	1 Feb 1992	400	4 years					
4/K	Kiln	1 Sep 1992	900	6 years					
3/W	Wheel	1 Mar 1994	420	4 years					
Totals									
Disposals									
Totals c/f									

MOTOR VEHICLES									
Ref	Description	Date of purchase	Cost £	Depreciation type	Accumulated depreciation 31 Dec 1995 £	Date of disposal	Net book value 31 Dec 1995 £	Sale/scrap proceeds £	Loss/ profit £
1/V	Van reg G249 NPO	1 Feb 1990	4000	Reducing balance 25%					
2/V	Van reg K697 JKL	1 June 1993	6000	Reducing balance 25%					
3/V	Van reg M894 TMG	30 Sep 1994	8000	Reducing balance 25%					
Totals									
Disposals									
Totals c/f									

Practice devolved assessment

2 *Booths*

Performance criteria

The following performance criteria are covered in this Devolved Assessment.

Element 4.1: Maintain records and accounts relating to capital acquisition and disposal

1   Relevant details relating to capital expenditure are correctly entered in the appropriate records

Element 4.2: Record income and expenditure

1   All income and expenditure is correctly identified and recorded in the appropriate records

2   Relevant accruals and prepaid income and expenditure are correctly identified and adjustments are made

3   The organisation's policies, regulations, procedures and timescales are observed in relation to recording income and expenditure

Notes on completing the Assessment

This Assessment is designed to test your ability to post transactions correctly to the ledger accounts and the trial balance.

You are provided with data (Pages 48 to 57) which you must use to complete the tasks on Page 57.

You are allowed **two hours** to complete your work.

A high level of accuracy is required. Check your work carefully.

Correcting fluid should not be used. Errors should be crossed out neatly and clearly. You should write in ink and not in pencil.

A full suggested solution to this Assessment is provided on Page 127.

Do not turn to the suggested solution until you have completed all parts of the Assessment.

PRACTICE DEVOLVED ASSESSMENT 2: BOOTHS

Data

You are acting as the temporary bookkeeper at Booths Ltd, a builder's merchant. The financial year end, 30 June 19X7, is approaching. During the day of 30 June 19X7, several primary documents are passed to you for posting to the ledger accounts.

All sales and all purchases are made on credit. All other expenses are paid *immediately* on receipt of a bill.

The ledger accounts appear as follows at the end of 29 June 19X7.

ADVERTISING					
19X7			19X7		
29 June Balance b/f	288	91			

ACCOUNTANCY FEES					
19X7			19X7		
29 June Balance b/f	1,500	00			

BANK ACCOUNT					
19X7			19X7		
29 June Balance b/f	19,330	65			

DOUBTFUL DEBT PROVISION					
19X7			19X7		
			29 June Balance b/f	1,242	94

ELECTRICITY					
19X7			19X7		
29 June Balance b/f	1,733	84			

FIXTURES AND FITTINGS					
19X7			19X7		
29 June Balance b/f	11,893	55			

GAS					
19X7			19X7		
29 June Balance b/f	1,161	20			

INSURANCE					
19X7			19X7		
29 June Balance b/f	658	38			

INTEREST					
19X7			19X7		
29 June Balance b/f	1,141	31			

MAINTENANCE					
19X7			19X7		
29 June Balance b/f	3,807	43			

MOTOR EXPENSES					
19X7			19X7		
29 June Balance b/f	606	19			

MOTOR VEHICLES					
19X7			19X7		
29 June Balance b/f	43,675	07			

PROFIT AND LOSS ACCOUNT					
19X7			19X7		
			29 June Balance b/f	27,225	92

PURCHASES					
19X7			19X7		
29 June Balance b/f	76,648	31			

PURCHASE LEDGER CONTROL A/C					
19X7			19X7		
			29 June Balance b/f	9,554	93

PRINT, POSTAGE & STATIONERY					
19X7			19X7		
29 June Balance b/f	117	29			

RENT					
19X7			19X7		
29 June Balance b/f	9,250	00			

SHARE CAPITAL					
19X7			19X7		
			29 June Balance b/f	10,000	00

ACCUMULATED DEPRECIATION					
19X7			19X7		
			29 June Balance b/f	27,241	12

SALES					
19X7			19X7		
			29 June Balance b/f	180,754	17

SALES LEDGER CONTROL A/C					
19X7			19X7		
29 June Balance b/f	19,356	30			

SUNDRY EXPENSES					
19X7			19X7		
29 June Balance b/f	1,427	70			

OPENING STOCK					
19X7			19X7		
29 June Balance b/f	37,321	56			

TELEPHONE					
19X7			19X7		
29 June Balance b/f	3,879	09			

UNIFIED BUSINESS RATE					
19X7			19X7		
29 June Balance b/f	4,917	94			

VAT CONTROL A/C					
19X7			19X7		
			29 June Balance b/f	6,719	19

WAGES					
19X7			19X7		
29 June Balance b/f	21,575	63			

WATER RATES					
19X7			19X7		
29 June Balance b/f	2,447	92			

The documents which have been passed to you are as follows:

BOOTHS LTD	62 Maple St NO7 3PN Tax point 30.06.X7 VAT No. 3171156327

MP Price & Co A/C No. 01729	Q	£
Standard bricks	400	504.00
TOTAL		504.00
VAT 17.5%		88.20
		£592.20

BOOTHS LTD	62 Maple St NO7 3PN Tax point 30.06.X7 VAT No. 3171156327

H Contractors A/C No. 02147	Q	£
Cement bags	10	67.00
Trowel	1	5.50
Spirit Level	1	17.95
TOTAL		90.45
VAT 17.5%		15.83
		£106.28

BOOTHS LTD	62 Maple St NO7 3PN Tax point 30.06.X7 VAT No. 3171156327

NP Plumbers A/C No. 01227	Q	£
Piping: 1 metre length	40	210.00
Piping: 0.5 metre length	40	102.00
'A' type fittings	25	30.75
TOTAL		342.75
VAT 17.5%		59.98
		402.73

BOOTHS LTD	62 Maple St NO7 3PN Tax point 30.06.X7 VAT No. 3171156327

CR Harris & Co A/C No. 03994	Q	£
Standard bricks	500	630.00
White bricks	50	100.00
TOTAL		730.00
VAT 17.5%		127.75
		857.75

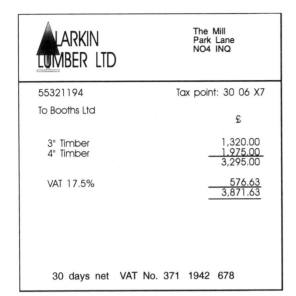

LARKIN
LUMBER LTD

The Mill
Park Lane
NO4 INQ

55321194   Tax point: 30 06 X7

To Booths Ltd
                                        £

    3" Timber   1,320.00
    4" Timber   1,975.00
                                 3,295.00

    VAT 17.5%   576.63
                                 3,871.63

    30 days net   VAT No. 371 1942 678

Tax point	Inv. no.
3006X7	X371172L

PLUMBING SUPPLIES LTD
Unit 17 Park Estate No7 1ZR

To Booths Ltd

        4cm piping   20m   486.23
        6cm piping   30m   1,049.82

TOTAL   1,536.05
VAT   268.81
Amount due   1,804.86

        VAT No. 442 1986 883   30 days net

                    Post Office Counters Ltd
                    Tax point: 30 07 X7

To Booths Ltd

Franking services
01 March 19X7 to 31 May 19X7

869   1st   208.56
942   2nd   169.56

                                 378.12

            HALFWAY INVESTMENTS LIMITED

To Booths Ltd   Tax point 29 June 19X7
                       VAT 497 3328 679

RENT

QUARTER TO
29 September 19X7   £2,312.50

WOODLEY GAZETTE
37 Half Lane
NO7 9RP

INV 21737

Tax point: 30/6/X7

VAT No. 113 4279 179

Booths Ltd Wednesday 5th June Half page ad.	33.50
VAT @ 17.5%	5.86
Total	39.36

007321

M Able & Co
Insurance Brokers
9 Green Lane
NO3 4PW

Tax point
30.06.19X7

To Booths Ltd
62 Maple St

Motor vehicle
insurance
per attatched

£1,437.50

Year to 31 May 19X8. Sorry
for the delay - you have
still been covered

Pratts Garage
114 Lark Road
NO1 1NR

S14117

Tax point: 30/6/X7

VAT No. 172 1173 499

BOOTHS LTD A/C 4173

Petrol and oil to 30 June 19X7	317.42
VAT @ 17.5%	55.55
	372.97

I134734

IRT DEALERS
4 The Forecourt

To: Booths Ltd
62 Maple St
NO7 3PN

VAT 147 3321 198
Tax point: 30/6/X7

Executive Car XZ3i Reg J172 BNC	12,600.00
Road Tax	100.00
Extras	542.75
	13,242.75
VAT £13,142.75 @ 17.5%	2,299.98
	15,542.73

```
        ╱╲
       ╱  ╲       NATIONAL
      ╱╲  ╱╲      ELECTRICITY
     ╱  ╲╱  ╲
```

YOUR CUSTOMER SERVICES OFFICE IS:	YOU CAN PHONE US ON:
POWER ROAD LONDON E2 9AJ	0171 123 1234

BOOTHS LTD
62 MAPLE STREET
NO7 3PN

WHEN TELEPHONING
We have a call queuing system. When you hear the ringing tone please wait for a reply as calls are answered in strict rotation.
BUSY TIMES
Please try to avoid 9-30AM - 10-30 AM and 2 PM to 3 PM

METER READING		UNITS USED	UNIT PRICE (pence)	V.A.T code	AMOUNT £
PRESENT	PREVIOUS				
31946E	29587	2359	17.470	1	412.12
STANDING CHARGE				1	217.50
TOTAL CHARGE (EXCLUDING VAT)					629.62
VAT 1 629.62 @ 17.5% COMMERCIAL					110.18

MAKE YOUR BILLS EASIER TO SWALLOW - SEE PAGE 4 OF `SOURCE'

DIRECT DEBIT
THE EASY WAY TO PAY

E=Estimated reading. Please read carefully the advice given on the back of this bill
C=Your own reading

BALANCE TO PAY			739.80
VAT CHARGE THIS BILL			110.18

YOUR ACCOUNT NUMBER	BILL DATE/TAX POINT	READING DATE	NON-DOMESTIC USE
34721193672	29.06.X7	29.06.X7	100%

You have also received the following information.

(a) Bank interest of £67.48 has been charged on the company's bank account but has not yet been posted.

(b) The gross wages cost for June, paid on 30 June 19X7, amounted to £2,169.52.

Tasks

(a) Post the transactions shown above to the ledger accounts.

(b) Balance and close off the ledger accounts. You should balance off the revenue and expenditure accounts (as well as the asset and liability accounts), but there is no need to post the balances to the profit and loss account.

(c) Post the balances in the ledger accounts to the trial balance provided overleaf. Add up the trial balance to check that it balances. Investigate any discrepancies.

Note. For (a) to (c) ignore accruals and prepayments.

(d) Identify any accruals and prepayments which would require adjustment in the *extended* trial balance.

Folio	Account	Ref	Trial balance	
			Debit	Credit
			£	£
	TOTAL			
Folio	Account	Ref		

Practice devolved assessment

3   *Lakeland Catering*

Performance criteria

The following performance criteria are covered in this Devolved Assessment.

Element 4.1: Maintain records and accounts relating to capital acquisition and disposal

1   Relevant details relating to capital expenditure are correctly entered in the appropriate records

4   Depreciation charges and other necessary entries and adjustments are correctly calculated and recorded in the appropriate records

---

Element 4.2: Record income and expenditure

4   Incomplete data is identified and either resolved or referred to the appropriate person

---

Element 4.4: Prepare the extended trial balance

1   Totals from the general ledger or other records are correctly entered on the ETB

2   Adjustments not dealt with in the ledger accounts are correctly entered on the ETB

4   An agreed valuation of closing work is correctly entered on the ETB

7   The ETB is accurately extended and totalled

Notes on completing the Assessment

This Assessment is designed to test your ability to record capital transactions, prepare accounts from incomplete records and prepare the extended trial balance.

You are provided with data (Pages 60 to 62) which you must use to complete the tasks on Pages 60 and 61.

You are allowed **four hours** in total to complete your work.

A high level of accuracy is required. Check your work carefully.

Correcting fluid should not be used. Errors should be crossed out neatly and clearly. You should write in ink and not in pencil.

A full suggested solution to this Assessment is provided on Page 135.

Do not turn to the suggested solution until you have completed all parts of the Assessment.

PRACTICE DEVOLVED ASSESSMENT 3: LAKELAND CATERING

Background information

Lakeland Catering is an organisation established by David Newsome in the early 1990s and which specialises in two main trading activities as follows:

1 Day to day catering operated through a shop and restaurant
2 Specialist catering for functions and banquets

The business which started in a small way has expanded quite rapidly and now employs 18 staff on either a full time or a part time basis.

David has been finding it increasingly difficult to find time to deal with the day to day paperwork and bookkeeping and has appointed you (Caroline Carter) to help him keep day to day control of the organisation's finances and produce some of the necessary financial year end figures for the organisation's accountant.

It is now 31 January 1997 and the firm's year end is 31 December.

In order to complete the tasks you will find attached the following items.

Shop and restaurant

1 Memorandum from David relating to the shop and restaurant

2 List of balances as at 1 January 1996

3 Cash book information for 1996

4 Statement of affairs proforma

5 Closing cash position proforma

6 Control account proformas

7 Trading and profit and loss account proforma

8 Balance sheet proforma

Specialist catering

1 Memorandum from David relating to vans

2 Depreciation methods memorandum proforma

3 Straight line depreciation calculation proforma

4 Reducing balance depreciation calculation proforma

5 Note from David relating to the extended trial balance as at 31 December 1996

6 Extended trial balance proforma

Tasks

Shop and restaurant

(a) Prepare an opening statement of affairs as at 1 January 1996 clearly identifying the Capital account balance at 1 January 1996.

(b) Calculate the cash position as at 31 December 1996.

(c) Prepare the following control accounts.

    (i)   Trade debtors (credit sales only)
    (ii)   Trade creditors
    (iii) Rent
    (iv) Wages
    (v)   Electricity

(d) Prepare the trading and profit and loss account for the period ended 31 December 1996.

(e) Prepare the balance sheet as at 31 December 1996.

Specialist catering

(f) Write a short note to David on the attached proforma, explaining the difference between straight line and reducing balance methods of depreciation.

(g) Calculate the fixed asset records for the van using the proforma and the straight line method of depreciation.

(h) Calculate the fixed asset records for the van using the proforma and, as an alternative, a reducing balance of 40% method of depreciation.

(i) Extend the trial balance, calculate the profit or loss, and balance the extended trial balance.

MEMORANDUM

To: Caroline
From: David
Date: 31 January 1997

Shop and restaurant

As you are aware I have had some difficulty keeping up to date with all the necessary records and bookkeeping and so unfortunately I have not kept a complete set of records.

I have managed though to put together some information which I am enclosing as follows.

(a) Balances at 1 January 1996
(b) Cash book information for 1996.

Shop and restaurant

List of balances 1 January 1996

	£
Stock	6,000
Debtors	200
Creditors	1,100
Vehicle (NBV)	5,800
Restaurant fittings (NBV)	3,900
Rent owing	250
Wages owing	610
Electricity prepayment	150
Cash at bank	350

Cash book information for 1996

	£		£
Balance 1 January 1996	350	Payments to trade creditors	17,850
Receipts from debtors	4,910	Telephone	570
Cash sales	27,060	Restaurant maintenance	710
		Insurance	312
		Rent	745
		Wages	8,090
		Electricity	640

All cash and cheques had been banked.

The following needs to be taken into account.

(a) At 31 December 1996 £250 was owing for electricity and £60 rent was paid in advance.

(b) Fittings are depreciated at 20% and the vehicle at 30%, both on a reducing balance basis.

(c) Balances at 31 December 1996 were as follows:

	£
Debtors	615
Creditors	840
Stock	5,400

Shop and restaurant

For task (a)

Statement of affairs as at 1 January 1996

	£	£

Assets

Less: liabilities

For task (b)

Closing cash position as at 31 December 1996

£   £

Receipts

Payments

Closing cash book balance

For task (c)

Control accounts
Trade debtors

	£		£

Trade creditors

	£		£

Rent

	£		£

Wages

	£		£

Electricity

	£		£

For task (d)

Shop and restaurant
Trading and profit and loss account for the period ended 31 December 1996

	£	£

For task (e)

Shop and restaurant
Balance sheet as at 31 December 1996

	£	£	£

MEMORANDUM

To: Caroline
From: David
Date: 31 January 1997

Specialist catering - vans

I have recently been reviewing the use of vans for our specialist catering division. I do not really understand depreciation but our accountant tells me that we should change our depreciation method from straight line to reducing balance, whatever that means.

The current van we use in the specialist catering division was bought on 1 January 1996 for £10,000 and it was estimated that it would have a useful life of six years, at the end of which it could be sold for £460. Depreciation was to be provided on a straight line basis.

The accountant informs me that the same van, if depreciated on a reducing balance basis would now have a different value in the business. This I do not understand.

For task (f)

MEMORANDUM

To: David
From: Caroline
Date: 31 January 1997

Depreciation methods

MEMORANDUM (cont'd)

For task (g)

Van depreciation - straight line method

Depreciation charge $= \dfrac{10,000 - 460}{6} = 1,590$

		Depreciation charge for year £	Book value £
End of year	1		
	2		
	3		
	4		
	5		
	6		

For task (h)

Van depreciation - reducing balance method

Cost = £10,000

		Calculation of depreciation charge £	Depreciation charge for year £	Book value £
End of year	1			
	2			
	3			
	4			
	5			
	6			

MEMORANDUM

To: Caroline
From: David
Date: 31 January 1997

Extended trial balance

Please can you complete the extended trial balance for the specialist catering division. I've made a start on it, but I know the following adjustments have still got to be put through.

(a) Vehicle depreciation   £1,590

(b) Fittings depreciation   £250

(c) Electricity owing   £100

(d) Rent prepayment   £250

(e) An invoice of £50 has been charged to insurance when it should have been charged to telephone.

(f) Closing stock at 31 December 1996 of £3,000.

For task (i)

LAKELAND CATERING - SPECIALIST CATERING DIVISION

Description	Trial balance Debit £	Trial balance Credit £	Adjustments Debit £	Adjustments Credit £	Accruals £	Pre-payments £	Profit and loss account Debit £	Profit and loss account Credit £	Balance sheet Debit £	Balance sheet Credit £
Sales		38,500								
Purchases	19,250									
Opening stock	4,000									
Wages	10,100									
Electricity	750									
P/L Depn -fittings										
-vehicles										
Telephone	600									
Insurance	450									
Rent	950									
Fixtures - cost	5,000									
depn		2,500								
Vehicle - cost	10,000									
depn										
Stock - bal sheet										
trading a/c										
Debtors	700									
Creditors		1,200								
Cash in hand	100									
Bank over-draft		1,400								
Capital		8,300								
Prepayments										
Accruals										
Net profit										
	51,900	51,900								

Practice devolved assessment
4 Cut Price Electricals

Performance criteria

The following performance criteria are covered in this Devolved Assessment.

Element 4.1: Maintain records and accounts relating to capital acquisition and disposal

1   Relevant details relating to capital expenditure are correctly entered in the appropriate records

4   Depreciation charges and other necessary entries and adjustments are correctly calculated and recorded in the appropriate records

6   Profit or loss on disposal is correctly calculated and recorded in the accounts

Element 4.2: Record income and expenditure

4   Incomplete data is identified and either resolved or referred to the appropriate person

Element 4.4: Prepare the extended trial balance

1   Totals from the general ledger or other records are correctly entered on the ETB

3   Adjustments not dealt with in the ledger accounts are correctly entered on the ETB

4   An agreed valuation of closing work is correctly entered on the ETB

7   The ETB is accurately extended and totalled

Notes on completing the Assessment

This Assessment is designed to test your ability to record capital transactions, prepare accounts from incomplete records and prepare the extended trial balance.

You are provided with data (Pages 74 to 76) which you must use to complete the tasks on Pages 74 and 75.

You are allowed **four hours** in total to complete your work.

A high level of accuracy is required. Check your work carefully.

Correcting fluid should not be used. Errors should be crossed out neatly and clearly. You should write in ink and not in pencil.

A full suggested solution to this Assessment is provided on Page 141.

Do not turn to the suggested solution until you have completed all parts of the Assessment.

PRACTICE DEVOLVED ASSESSMENT 4: CUT PRICE ELECTRICALS

Background information

Cut Price Electricals is a medium sized organisation in the North of England specialising in two major areas of activity:

(a)   Electrical products - wholesaling and retailing
(b)   Electrical installation and contracting

The two aspects of the business are treated as separate for accounting purposes although both parts belong to the same business organisation.

The business was established in the mid 1980's by Ian McFarland who retired around 5 years ago leaving the day to day control of the business to his niece Karen Wiggans.

The business has been expanding rapidly over the last few years and Karen has increasingly needed to spend time away from the business attending trade fairs and negotiating contracts. In view of this, and given the significant amount of work which needs doing in establishing and maintaining the financial controls and systems within the organisation, she has recently appointed you (Peter Phillips) as an Accounting Technician to help her with the bookkeeping and the accounting.

It is now 30 November 1996 and the company's year end is 31 October.

Karen is extremely busy and has just left for a three week tour of major trade fairs in the South of England. She has had to leave you alone to put together some of the adjustments and records needed in preparing the accounts for the year ended 31 October 1996. You have been supplied with a certain amount of information which will help you with the more immediate tasks.

In order to complete the tasks, you will find attached the following items:

Retailing Division

(a)   Memorandum from Karen Wiggans relating to the Retailing Division
(b)   Proforma for opening capital statement
(c)   Control account proformas
(d)   Bank Reconciliation proforma
(e)   Memorandum from Karen Wiggans relating to depreciation of vans
(f)   Proforma for van depreciation and fixed asset disposal

Installation and contracting

(a)   Memorandum from Karen Wiggans relating to the trial balance as at 31 October
(b)   Extended trial balance proforma

Tasks

Retail Division

(a)   Prepare a statement of opening capital for the Retail Division, as at 1 November 1995, in the form of a Trial Balance.

(b)   Prepare the following control accounts

  (i)   Wages
  (ii)   Rent
  (iii)   Rates
  (iv)   Advertising
  (v)   Insurance
  (vi)   Debtors (trade) - not to include cash sales
  (vii)   Creditors (trade) - not to include cash purchases

(c)   Prepare a bank reconciliation statement for Mrs Wiggans.

(d)   Complete the asset register for Van number 2.

(e)   Complete the following accounts for the disposal of Van number 1.

  (i)   Van account
  (ii)   Van depreciation account
  (iii)   Asset disposal account

Installation and Contracting Division

(f)   Enter the balances as at 31 October 1996 onto the attached proforma.

(g)   Make any adjustments necessary, following the memorandum from Karen Wiggans, onto the trial balance.

(h)   Extend the trial balance, calculate the profit or loss, and balance the extended trial balance.

MEMORANDUM

To: Peter Phillips

From: Karen Wiggans

Date: 30/11/96

Retailing Division

Welcome to Cut Price Electricals!

I am sorry that I have to leave you alone so soon after joining Cut Price Electricals but as you know, I am on a three week tour of the major trade fairs in the South of England.

There are several urgent tasks which need doing in connection with our Retailing Division to help prepare the necessary books and records prior to completion of our annual accounts.

I have managed to gather some information which should help you with these tasks and this I set out below.

(a)   The following balances are available

		1 November 1995 £'000	31 October 1996 £'000
Premises	- cost	100	100
	- depreciation	20	20
Fixtures	- cost	85	85
	- depreciation	15	15
Stock		36	46
Debtors (trade)		20	14
Creditors (trade)		16	27
Vans	- cost	20	20
	- depreciation	10	10
Wages in advance		2	5
Rent in advance		7	3
Rates in arrears		6	2
Insurance - in advance		6	-
Insurance - in arrears		-	3
Advertising - in arrears		5	8

(b)   A summary of the cash book shows the following for the year ended 31/10/96

		£'000
Receipts		
Cash in hand - 1/11/95		2
Debtors		212
Cash sales		37
Payments		
Bank overdraft - 1/11/95		7
Creditor payments (trade)		104
Cash purchases		12
Wages		79
Rent		17
Rates		14
Advertising		8
Insurance		16
Miscellaneous		24

All cash is banked at the earliest opportunity.

(c)   Mr Shah, our bank manager, has told me that we were significantly overdrawn on 31/10/96. I have looked at our cash book and checked it against the bank statement and the differences seem to be as follows.

(i)   Income not yet credited to bank statement but in cash book is £17,000.

(ii) Cheques paid out of our cash book figures but not yet charged to our account:

101202	£900
101206	£1,100
101209	£650

There was no cash in hand at the year end because I ensured that it was all banked as soon as it was received.

For task (a)

Cut Price Electricals retail division opening capital statement as at 1 November 1995

	DR	CR
	£'000	£'000

For task (a)

Cut Price Electricals retail division opening capital statement as at 1 November 1995

	DR	CR
	£'000	£'000

For task (b)

Control accounts - Retail division

Wages

	£'000		£'000

Rent

	£'000		£'000

Rates

	£'000		£'000

For task (b) (continued)

Advertising

£'000		£'000

Insurance

£'000		£'000

Trade debtors

£'000		£'000

For task (b) (continued)

Trade creditors

	£'000		£'000

For task (c)

**Cut Price Electricals
Bank Reconciliation Statement**

£

Balance as per bank statement

Unlodged credits

Uncleared cheques

Balance as per cash book

MEMORANDUM

To: Peter Phillips

From: Karen Wiggans

Date: 30/11/96

Depreciation of Vans

The Retailing Division has 2 vans, details of which are set out below.

Figures have been rounded and at the end of 1994/95, the NBV of both vans was £10,000. Depreciation needs adding for both vans for 1995/96. The depreciation rate for both vans will be 20% straight-line basis assuming no residual value.

You will not be aware that I have been considering selling van number 1 and the offer I received of £3,500 just before the year end I have now accepted. There was no estimated residual value for this van.

Retailing Division
Van Records

Van no	Purchased	Cost £	Depreciation to 31/10/95 £	NBV £
1	1992/93	10,000	(6,000)	4,000
2	1993/94	10,000	(4,000)	6,000

For task (d)

Fixed asset register as at 31 October 1996
Van Number 2

Cost £	Depreciation to 31/10/95 £	Depreciation for year ended 31/10/96 £	Net book value at 31/10/96 £

For task (e)

Van number 1

Van account

	£'000		£'000

Van depreciation account

	£'000		£'000

Asset disposal account

	£'000		£'000

MEMORANDUM

To: Peter Phillips

From: Karen Wiggans

Date: 30/11/96

Installation and Contracting

I have managed to obtain the attached list of balances for the Installation and Contracting Division as at 31/10/96. You will need to take account of the following adjustments.

(a) Closing stock at 31/10/96 following the stocktaking was £14,000.

(b) Depreciation needs providing as follows:

   (i)   Vans - straight line method at 30% with no estimated residual value
   (ii) Fixtures - straight line method at 4% with no estimated residual value

(c) I would like to make a provision of £2,000 to cover possible bad debts.

(d) Rent on the garage includes a payment for the next financial year of £1,000.

(e) An invoice for £3,000 which has been charged to van expenses should have been charged to travel expenses.

(f) There is an outstanding advertising invoice for £2,000 for the year to 31/10/96.

Installation and contracting
Balances as at 31 October 1996

	£'000
Sales	109
Purchases	64
Stock (1/11/95)	11
Wages	57
Van expenses	14
Travel expenses	3
Garage rent	6
Insurance	2
Tools allowance	5
Advertising	8
Miscellaneous expenses	4
Vans - cost	20
Vans - depreciation	12
Fixtures - cost	75
Fixtures - depreciation	60
Capital	100
Debtors	36
Creditors	21
Cash in hand	6
Bank overdraft	9

For tasks (f), (g), (h)

CUT PRICE ELECTRICALS - INSTALLATION AND CONTRACTING DIVISION

Description	Trial balance		Adjustments		Accruals	Pre-payments	Profit and loss account		Balance sheet	
	Debit	Credit	Debit	Credit			Debit	Credit	Debit	Credit
	£'000	£'000	£'000	£'000	£'000	£'000	£'000	£'000	£'000	£'000

Trial run devolved assessment

TRIAL RUN DEVOLVED ASSESSMENT

INTERMEDIATE STAGE - NVQ/SVQ3

Unit 4

Maintaining financial records

and

Preparing accounts

The purpose of this Trial Run Devolved Assessment is to give you an idea of what a Devolved Assessment could be like. It is not intended as a definitive guide to the tasks you may be required to perform.

The suggested time allowance for this Assessment is four hours. Extra time may be permitted in a real Devolved Assessment. Breaks in assessment may be allowed, but it must normally be completed in one day.

Calculators may be used but no reference material is permitted.

**DO NOT OPEN THIS PAPER UNTIL YOU ARE READY TO START
UNDER TIMED CONDITIONS**

INSTRUCTIONS

This Assessment is designed to test your ability to record capital transactions and prepare financial accounts.

Background information is provided on Page 91.

The tasks you are to perform are set out on Page 91.

You are provided with data on Pages 92 to 94 which you must use to complete the tasks.

Your answers should be set out in the answer booklet on Pages 95 to 101 using the documents provided. You may require additional answer pages.

You are allowed **four hours** to complete your work.

A high level of accuracy is required. Check your work carefully.

Correcting fluid may not be used. Errors should be crossed out neatly and clearly. You should write in black ink, not pencil.

You are advised to read the whole of the Assessment before commencing as all of the information may be of value and is not necessarily supplied in the sequence in which you might wish to deal with it.

A full suggested solution to this Assessment is provided on Pages 147 to 154.

BACKGROUND INFORMATION

Gordon Blur Ltd manufactures and trades in high quality kitchenware for sale to trade and retail customers. The company was established in 19X2 and operates from leasehold premises in Holloway, North London.

Gordon Blur is the managing director and the chief accountant is Kit Shenett. You are the accounts clerk. You have started the job only recently: the previous accounts clerk, Karen Taddup left suddenly having made a few errors and omissions.

The firm is rather old fashioned and still uses a manual accounting system and fixed assets register.

Kit Shenett has gone on holiday leaving you with a trial balance which needs adjusting, a fixed assets register which needs updating and a memo with various pieces of information.

TASKS TO BE COMPLETED

In the answer booklet on Pages 95 to 101 complete the tasks outlined below for the year ended 31 December 19X6. Data for this assessment is provided on Pages 92 to 94.

(a) Enter all the information relating to fixed assets in the ledger accounts given, the journal and the fixed assets register.

(b) Show the journal entries required for items (b) and (c) in the memorandum.

(c) Enter the opening trial balance on the attached proforma after making any adjustments in connection with fixed assets, including recording the profit or loss on the sale of the van.

(d) Make any other adjustments required arising from journal entries, accruals or prepayments on the ETB.

(e) Extend the trial balance, calculate the profit and balance the ETB.

DATA

In order to complete the tasks listed on the previous page you should find attached the following items.

(a) Memorandum from Kit Shenett with some information and helpful hints.
(b) Trial balance as at 31 December 19X6.
(c) Relevant pages of fixed asset register as at 31 December 19X5 (ie last year).

MEMORANDUM

To: Accounts Clerk
From: Kit Shenett
Date: 31 December 19X6

Please find attached a trial balance as at 31 December 19X6. Before the final accounts can be prepared there are several adjustments which need to be made. You will need to do these through the journal, and the extended trial balance (proformas attached).

(a) Could you update the fixed assets register? I always like to ensure that the fixed assets register is kept up to date. Your predecessor Karen didn't do this, omitting to record the fact that on 3 August 19X6 the old van (Reg F396 HJB) was traded in for a new one (K125 ATE) costing £12,000. We were given a trade in allowance of £2,000 on the old van, the balance to be paid later in 19X7 and to be included for now in sundry creditors.

No depreciation has been provided on fixed assets. Could you make the appropriate entries in the journal and adjust the trial balance for this and for the purchase and sale of the vans?

You may find it helpful to use the attached ledger accounts to calculate the profit or loss on disposal of the van. You will need to open an account to record this in the ETB.

Don't forget - plant and equipment is depreciated on the straight line basis over the periods shown in the fixed assets register. Leasehold property is amortised over the period of the lease and motor vehicles are depreciated using the reducing balance method at 25% per annum. We charge a full year's depreciation in the year of purchase and none in the year of sale.

(b) The suspense account balance consists of £4,770 which was money spent on repairs to the equipment. Karen was not very good at understanding the difference between capital and revenue expenditure, so she did not know where to put it. I take it you know where it should go!

(c) One of our customers, a Mr D Faults, has gone into liquidation owing us £200. We also need to increase the bad debts provision to 5% of net trade debtors.

(d) As you probably know, stock at 31.12.X6 is valued at £10,412.

(e) The audit fee of £1,500 needs to be accrued under accounting fees.

(f) We have paid some wages in advance to Luke Easword, amounting to £600.

(g) Our last electricity bill was dated 31 October and was for £300, the normal quarterly charge.

GORDON BLUR LIMITED
TRIAL BALANCE AS AT 31 DECEMBER 19X6

Folio		Dr £	Cr £
P110	Plant and equipment (cost)	55,330	
P120	Plant and equipment (provision for depreciation)		39,660
P130	Plant and equipment (depreciation expense)	-	
M110	Motor vehicles (cost)	25,500	
M120	Motor vehicles (provision for depreciation)		10,788
M130	Motor vehicles (depreciation expense)	-	
L110	Leasehold premises (cost)	100,000	
L120	Leasehold premises (accumulated amortisation)		8,000
L130	Leasehold premises (amortisation expense)	-	
C300	Sundry creditors		3,500
F100	Bank	6,132	
F200	Cash in hand	505	
A100	Accountancy fee	600	
B100	Bad debts provision		150
B200	Bad debts expense		
L300	Loan		10,000
R200	Repairs and maintenance	813	
M300	Motor expenses	1,506	
S100	Sales		205,806
D100	Trade debtors	50,287	
P100	Purchases	158,142	
C100	Trade creditors		65,416
E100	Electricity	900	
P300	Printing, postage, stationery	3,717	
P200	Profit and loss account		40,956
S200	Stock at 1.1.X6	9,125	
S300	Share capital		100,000
S400	Suspense account	4,770	
S500	Sundry expenses	6,428	
W100	Wages and salaries	60,521	
		484,276	484,276

FIXED ASSET REGISTER AS AT 31 DECEMBER 19X5

PLANT AND EQUIPMENT

Ref	Description	Date of purchase	Cost £	Depreciation period	Accumulated depreciation 31.12.X5 £	Date of disposal	Net book value 31.12.X5 £	Sale/scrap proceeds £	(Loss)/ profit £
P111	Cutter	1.3.X2	24,750	5 years	19,800		4,950		
P112	Moulding machine	2.5.X3	12,300	6 years	6,150		6,150		
P113	Assembler	6.6.X3	18,280	4 years	13,710		4,570		
Totals			55,330		39,660		15,670		

MOTOR VEHICLES

Ref	Description	Date of purchase	Cost £	Depreciation type	Accumulated depreciation 31.12.X5 £	Date of disposal	Net book value 31.12.X5 £	Sale/scrap proceeds £	(Loss)/ profit £
M111	Van reg F396 HJB	22.2.X2	6,500	Reducing balance 25%	4,444		2,056		
M112	Van reg H842 GSL	17.3.X4	8,500	Reducing balance 25%	3,719		4,781		
M113	Van reg J542 KLH	12.9.X5	10,500	Reducing balance 25%	2,625		7,875		
Totals			25,500		10,788		14,712		

LEASEHOLD PREMISES

Ref	Description	Date of purchase	Cost £	Term of lease	Accumulated amortisation 31.12.X5 £	Date of disposal	Net book value 31.12.X5 £	Disposal proceeds £	(Loss)/ profit £
L110	Leasehold property	1.1.X2	100,000	50 years	8,000		92,000		

TRIAL RUN DEVOLVED ASSESSMENT

Maintaining financial records

and

Preparing accounts

ANSWER BOOKLET

In this answer booklet you should find attached the following documents on which to complete the tasks.

(a) Partially completed fixed asset register as at 31 December 19X6 for updating
(b) Pages of the journal
(c) Extended trial balance proformas
(d) Ledger account proformas relating to fixed assets

FIXED ASSET REGISTER AS AT 31 DECEMBER 19X6

PLANT AND EQUIPMENT

Ref	Description	Date of purchase	Cost £	Depreciation period	Accumulated depreciation 31.12.X6 £	Date of disposal	Net book value 31.12.X6 £	Sale/scrap proceeds £	(Loss)/ profit £
P111	Cutter	1.3.X2	24,750	5 years					
P112	Moulding machine	2.5.X3	12,300	6 years					
P113	Assembler	6.6.X3	18,280	4 years					
Totals			55,330						

MOTOR VEHICLES

Ref	Description	Date of purchase	Cost £	Depreciation type	Accumulated depreciation 31.12.X6 £	Date of disposal	Net book value 31.12.X6 £	Sale/scrap proceeds £	(Loss)/ profit £
M111	Van reg 4396 HJB	22.2.X2	6,500	Reducing balance 25%					
M112	Van reg H842 GSL	17.3.X4	8,500	Reducing balance 25%					
M113	Van reg J542 KLH	12.9.X5	10,500	Reducing balance 25%					
Totals Disposals									
Totals									

LEASEHOLD PREMISES

Ref	Description	Date of purchase	Cost £	Term of lease	Accumulated amortisation 31.12.X6 £	Net book value 31.12.X6 £	Disposal proceeds £	(Loss)/ profit £
L110	Leasehold property	1.1.X2	100,000	50 years				

JOURNAL				Page 20
Date	Details	Folio Ref	£	£

BPP Publishing

Date	Details	Folio Ref	£	£

JOURNAL — Page 21

Folio	Account	Trial balance		Adjustments		Accrued	Prepaid	Profit and loss a/c		Balance sheet	
		Debit £	Credit £	Debit £	Credit £	£	£	Debit £	Credit £	Debit £	Credit £
	SUB-TOTAL										
	Profit for the year										
	TOTAL										

LEDGER ACCOUNTS

MOTOR VEHICLES

	£		£
Date			
19X6			
1 Jan Balance b/d	25,500		

MOTOR VEHICLES: PROVISION FOR DEPRECIATION

	£		£
		Date	
		19X6	
		1 Jan Balance b/d	10,788

MOTOR VEHICLES: DISPOSALS

	£		£

Solutions for Unit 4

SOLUTIONS TO SAMPLE SIMULATION

**DO NOT TURN THIS PAGE UNTIL YOU HAVE
COMPLETED THE SAMPLE SIMULATION**

SOLUTIONS TO SAMPLE SIMULATION: BRANSON & CO

EXTRACTS FROM FIXED ASSETS REGISTER

Tasks 1 and 2

Description/ serial no	Location	Date acquired	Original cost £	Enhance- ments £	Total £	Dep'n £	NBV £	Funding method	Disposal proceeds £	Disposal date
Plant and equipment										
Milling machine 45217809	Factory	20.6.94	3,456.08		3,456.08			Cash		
Y/e 31.3.95						864.02	2,592.06			
Y/e 31.3.96						864.02	1,728.04			
Y/e 31.3.97						864.02	864.02			
Y/e 31.3.98						864.02	0.00			
Lathe 299088071	Factory	12.6.95	4,008.24		4,008.24			Cash		
Y/e 31.3.96						1,002.06	3,006.18			
Y/e 31.3.97						1,002.06	2,004.12			
Y/e 31.3.98						1,002.06	1,002.06			
Drill assembly 51123412	Factory	12.2.96	582.44		582.44			Cash		
Y/e 31.3.96						145.61	436.83			
Y/e 31.3.97						145.61	291.22			
Y/e 31.3.98						145.61	145.61			
Punch drive 91775321	Factory	12.2.96	1,266.00		1,266.00			Cash plus trade-in		
Y/e 31.3.96						316.50	949.50			
Y/e 31.3.97						316.50	633.00			
Y/e 31.3.98						316.50	316.50			
Winding gear 53098871	Factory	13.3.96	1,082.68		1,082.68			Cash		
Y/e 31.3.96						270.67	812.01			
Y/e 31.3.97				341.79	1,153.80	384.60	769.20			
Y/e 31.3.98						384.60	384.60			
Tender press 44231809	Factory	8.8.96	4,256.04		4,256.04			Cash		
Y/e 31.3.97						1,064.01	3,192.03			
Y/e 31.3.98						1,064.01	2,128.02			

Description/ serial no	Location	Date acquired	Original cost £	Enhance- ments £	Total £	Dep'n £	NBV £	Funding method	Disposal proceeds £	Disposal date
Company cars										
M412 RTW	Yard	25.8.94	8,923.71		8,923.71			Lease		
Y/e 31.3.95						4,015.67	4,908.04			
Y/e 31.3.96						2,208.62	2,699.42			
Y/e 31.3.97						1,214.74	1,484.68			
Y/e 31.3.98						668.11	816.57			
M104 PTY	Yard	15.3.95	8,643.00		8,643.00			Cash		
Y/e 31.3.95						3,889.35	4,753.65			
Y/e 31.3.96						2,139.14	2,614.51			
Y/e 31.3.97						1,176.53	1,437.98			
Y/e 31.3.98									1,850.00	
N33 FGY	Yard	18.9.95	10,065.34		10,065.34			Cash plus trade-in		
Y/e 31.3.96						4,529.40	5,535.94			
Y/e 31.3.97						2,491.17	3,044.77			
Y/e 31.3.98						1,370.15	1,674.62			
P321 HDR	Yard	13.12.96	9,460.26		9,460.26			Cash		
Y/e 31.3.97						4,257.12	5,203.14			
Y/e 31.3.98						2,341.41	2,861.73			
R261 GHT	Yard	27.3.98	12,807.50		12,807.50			Cash plus trade-in		
Y/e 31.3.98						5,763.38	7,044.12			

Tasks 1, 2, 4, 6, 7

NOMINAL (GENERAL) LEDGER

Account   Administration overheads

Debit			**Credit**		
Date	*Details*	*Amount*	*Date*	*Details*	*Amount*
1998		£	1998		£
1 Mar	Balance b/f	15,071.23			
27 Mar	P/L control	140.00			
31 Mar	P/L control	991.24			
31 Mar	Bank	1,105.69	31 Mar	Balance c/d	17,308.16
		17,308.16			17,308.16
1 Apr	Balance b/d	17,308.16			

Account   Brandreth capital account

Debit			**Credit**		
Date	*Details*	*Amount*	*Date*	*Details*	*Amount*
1998		£	1998		£
			1 Mar	Balance b/f	17,063.24

Account   Brandreth current account

Debit			**Credit**		
Date	*Details*	*Amount*	*Date*	*Details*	*Amount*
1998		£	1998		£
1 Mar	Balance b/f	11,056.73			
31 Mar	Bank	500.00	31 Mar	Balance c/d	11,556.73
		11,556.73			11,556.73
1 Apr	Balance b/d	11,556.73			

Tasks 1, 2, 4, 6, 7 (continued)

Account	Company cars: cost				
Debit				Credit	
Date 1998	*Details*	*Amount* £	*Date* 1998	*Details*	*Amount* £
1 Mar 27 Mar	Balance b/f P/L control.	37,092.31 12,807.50 49,899.81	27 Mar 31 Mar	Disposal a/c Balance c/d	8,643.00 41,256.81 49,899.81
1 Apr	Balance b/d	41,256.81			

Account	Company cars: depreciation charge				
Debit				Credit	
Date 1998	*Details*	*Amount* £	*Date* 1998	*Details*	*Amount* £
31 Mar	Accumulated depreciation	10,143.05			

Account	Company cars: accumulated depreciation				
Debit				Credit	
Date 1997	*Details*	*Amount* £	*Date* 1997	*Details*	*Amount* £
			1 Apr	Balance b/f	25,921.74
1998 27 Mar 31 Mar	Disposal a/c Balance c/d	7,205.02 28,859.77 36,064.79	1998 31 Mar	Change for year	10,143.05 36,064.79
			1 Apr	Balance b/d	28,859.77

Tasks 1, 2, 4, 6, 7 (continued)

Account Debit	Company cars: disposals		Credit		
Date 1998	*Details*	*Amount* £	*Date* 1998	*Details*	*Amount* £
27 Mar	Cost	8,643.00	27 Mar	Accumulated depreciation	7,205.02
			27 Mar	Purchases ledger control account	1,850.00
31 Mar	Balance c/d	412.02			9,055.02
		9,055.02			
			1 Apr	Balance b/d	412.02

Account Debit	Direct labour costs		Credit		
Date 1998	*Details*	*Amount* £	*Date* 1998	*Details*	*Amount* £
1 Mar	Balance b/f	60,012.64			
31 Mar	Bank	6,014.73	31 Mar	Balance c/d	66,027.37
		66,027.37			66,027.37
1 Apr	Balance b/d	66,027.37			

Account Debit	Factory overheads		Credit		
Date 1998	*Details*	*Amount* £	*Date* 1998	*Details*	*Amount* £
1 Mar	Balance b/f	27,109.67			
31 Mar	P/L control	1,451.09			
31 Mar	Bank	1,931.75	31 Mar	Balance c/d	30,492.51
		30,492.51			30,492.51
1 Apr	Balance b/d	30,492.51			

Tasks 1, 2, 4, 6, 7 (continued)

Account Debit	Other fixed assets: cost		Credit		
Date 1998	*Details*	*Amount* £	*Date* 1998	*Details*	*Amount* £
1 Mar	Balance b/f	18,923.50			

Account Debit	Other fixed assets: depreciation charge		Credit		
Date 1998	*Details*	*Amount* £	*Date* 1998	*Details*	*Amount* £
31 Mar	Accumulated depreciation	4,730.88			

Account Debit	Other fixed assets: accumulated depreciation		Credit		
Date 1997	*Details*	*Amount* £	*Date* 1997	*Details*	*Amount* £
			1 Apr	Balance b/f	6,224.12
1998			1998		
			31 Mar	Charge for year	4,730.88
31 Mar	Balance c/d	10,955.00			
		10,955.00			10,955.00
			1 Apr	Balance b/d	10,955.00

Tasks 1, 2, 4, 6, 7 (continued)

Account	Other fixed assets: disposals				
Debit			Credit		
Date 1998	*Details*	*Amount* £	*Date* 1998	*Details*	*Amount* £

Account	Plant and equipment: cost				
Debit			Credit		
Date 1998	*Details*	*Amount* £	*Date* 1998	*Details*	*Amount* £
1 Mar	Balance b/f	14,993.27			

Account	Plant and equipment: depreciation charge				
Debit			Credit		
Date 1998	*Details*	*Amount* £	*Date* 1998	*Details*	*Amount* £
31 Mar	Accumulated depreciation	3,776.80			

Tasks 1, 2, 4, 6, 7 (continued)

Account Debit	Plant and equipment: accumulated depreciation		Credit		
Date 1997	*Details*	*Amount* £	*Date* 1997	*Details*	*Amount* £
			1 Apr	Balance b/f	7,239.68
1998 31 Mar	Balance c/d	11,016.48 <u>11,016.48</u>	1998 31 Mar	Charge for year	3,776.80 <u>11,016.48</u>
			1 Apr	Balance b/d	11,016.48

Account Debit	Plant and equipment: disposals		Credit		
Date 1998	*Details*	*Amount* £	*Date* 1998	*Details*	*Amount* £

Account Debit	Purchases		Credit		
Date 1998	*Details*	*Amount* £	*Date* 1998	*Details*	*Amount* £
1 Mar 31 Mar	Balance b/f P/L control	54,231.89 <u>4,871.22</u> <u>59,103.11</u>	31 Mar	Balance c/d	59,103.11 <u>59,103.11</u>
1 Apr	Balance b/d	59,103.11			

Tasks 1, 2, 4, 6, 7 (continued)

Account Debit	Purchases ledger control		Credit		
Date 1998	*Details*	*Amount* £	*Date* 1998	*Details*	*Amount* £
27 Mar	Car disposal a/c	1,850.00	1 Mar	Balance b/f	18,457.20
31 Mar	Bank	10,353.58	27 Mar	Purchase of new car	12,947.50
			31 Mar	Purchase invoices	
31 Mar	Balance c/d	28,334.30			9,133.18
		40,537.88			40,537.88
			1 Apr	Balance b/d	28,334.30

Account Debit	Sales		Credit		
Date 1998	*Details*	*Amount* £	*Date* 1998	*Details*	*Amount* £
			1 Mar	Balance b/f	225,091.42
31 Mar	Balance c/d	256,167.67	31 Mar	S/L control	31,076.25
		256,167.67			256,167.67
			1 Apr	Balance b/d	256,167.67

Account Debit	Sales ledger control		Credit		
Date 1998	*Details*	*Amount* £	*Date* 1998	*Details*	*Amount* £
1 Mar	Balance b/f	24,617.03	31 Mar	Bank	25,555.33
31 Mar	Sales invoices	36,514.59	31 Mar	Balance c/d	35,576.29
		61,131.62			61,131.62
1 Apr	Balance b/d	35,576.29			

Tasks 1, 2, 4, 6, 7 (continued)

Account Debit	Selling and distribution overheads		Credit		
Date 1998	*Details*	*Amount* £	*Date* 1998	*Details*	*Amount* £
1 Mar	Balance b/f	14,303.12			
31 Mar	P/L control	524.87			
31 Mar	Bank	1,427.88	31 Mar	Balance c/d	16,255.87
		16,255.87			16,255.87
1 Apr	Balance b/d	16,255.87			

Account Debit	Sondin capital account		Credit		
Date 1998	*Details*	*Amount* £	*Date* 1998	*Details*	*Amount* £
			1 Mar	Balance b/f	8,703.28

Account Debit	Sondin current account		Credit		
Date 1998	*Details*	*Amount* £	*Date* 1998	*Details*	*Amount* £
1 Mar	Balance b/f	12,912.29			
31 Mar	Bank	450.00	31 Mar	Balance c/d	13,362.29
		13,362.29			13,362.29
1 Apr	Balance b/d	13,362.29			

Tasks 1, 2, 4, 6, 7 (continued)

Account	Stock: raw materials				
Debit			Credit		
Date 1997	*Details*	*Amount* £	*Date* 1997	*Details*	*Amount* £
1 Apr	Balance b/f	6,294.33			

Account	Stock: finished goods				
Debit			Credit		
Date 1997	*Details*	*Amount* £	*Date* 1997	*Details*	*Amount* £
1 Apr	Balance b/f	12,513.77			

Account	Suspense				
Debit			Credit		
Date 1998	*Details*	*Amount* £	*Date* 1998	*Details*	*Amount* £
26 Jan	Bank	750.00	24 Feb	Bank	1,124.55
31 Mar	Balance c/d	374.55			
		1,124.55			1,124.55
			1 Apr	Balance b/d	374.55

Tasks 1, 2, 4, 6, 7 (continued)

Account	VAT				
Debit			Credit		
Date 1998	*Details*	*Amount* £	*Date* 1998	*Details*	*Amount* £
31 Mar	P/L control	1,294.76	1 Mar	Balance b/f	5,091.27
31 Mar	Balance c/d	9,234.85	31 Mar	S/L control	5,438.34
		10,529.61			10,529.61
			1 Apr	Balance b/d	9,234.85

Task 3

MEMORANDUM

To: Jenny Holden, Accountant

From: Val Denning, Accounts Assistant

Subject: Check on company cars at 31 March 1998

Date: 20 April 1998

I have compared the schedule of company cars actually on the premises at 31 March with the details in the fixed assets register. The only discrepancy is that the car M412 RTW was not on the premises, though listed in the register. I suggest that we check physical existence of this car at another time.

Task 5

Bank reconciliation as at 31 March 1998

	£	£
Balance per bank statement		(1,550.12) O/D
Outstanding lodgements		
27 March	6,071.88	
31 March	5,512.67	
		11,584.55
		10,034.43
Unpresented cheques		
19337	278.01	
19338	500.00	
19339	450.00	
		(1,228.01)
Balance per cash book		8,806.42

Tasks 7, 11, 12

Extended trial balance at 31 March 1998

Account name	Balances per ledger £	£	Adjustments £	£	Profit and loss account £	£	Balance sheet £	£
Administration overheads	17,308.16		420.00	1,625.00	16,103.16			
Brandreth capital account		17,063.24						17,063.24
Brandreth current account	11,556.73		750.00				12,306.73	
Company cars: cost	41,256.81						41,256.81	
Company cars: depreciation charge	10,143.05				10,143.05			
Company cars: accum depreciation		28,859.77						28,859.77
Company cars: disposals		412.02				412.02		
Direct labour costs	66,027.37				66,027.37			
Factory overheads	30,492.51				30,492.51			
Other fixed assets: cost	18,923.50			2,317.69			16,605.81	
Other fixed assets: depreciation charge	4,730.88				4,730.88			
Other fixed assets: accum depreciation		10,955.00	946.23					10,008.77
Other fixed assets: profit/loss on disposal			246.91		246.91			
Plant and equipment: cost	14,993.27						14,993.27	
Plant and equipment: depreciation charge	3,776.80				3,776.80			
Plant and equipment: accum depreciation		11,016.48						11,016.48
Purchases	59,103.11				59,103.11			
Purchases ledger control		28,334.30						28,334.30
Sales		256,167.67				256,167.67		
Sales ledger control	35,576.29						35,576.29	
Selling & distribution overheads	16,255.87				16,255.87			
Sondin: capital account		8,703.28						8,703.28
Sondin: current account	13,362.29						13,362.29	
Stock: raw materials	6,294.33		8,136.55	8,136.55	6,294.33	8,136.55	8,136.55	
Stock: finished goods	12,513.77		18,714.47	18,714.47	12,513.77	18,714.47	18,714.47	
Suspense		374.55	1,124.55	750.00				
VAT		9,234.85						9,234.85
Bank balance	8,806.42						8,806.42	
Accruals and prepayments			1,625.00	420.00			1,625.00	420.00
Net profit for the year					57,742.95			57,742.95
Total	371,121.16	371,121.16	31,963.71	31,963.71	283,430.71	283,430.71	171,383.64	171,383.64

Task 8

This cheque probably represents payment of a personal expense incurred by one or other of the partners. If so it will need to be treated as drawings.

To establish that this is so I will first ask Jenny Holden, the Accountant, whether she knows about the payment. If she does not, it may then be necessary for either she or I to inquire tactfully of the partners themselves.

Task 9

Journal

Date 1998	Account names and narrative	Debit £	Credit £
31 March	Brandreth: current account	750.00	
	suspense		750.00
	Being cash paid for personal expenses, classified as drawings		
31 March	Other fixed assets: accumulated depreciation	946.23	
	Other fixed assets: loss on disposal	246.91	
	Suspense account	1,124.55	
	Other fixed assets: cost		2,317.69
		2,317.69	2,317.69
	Being disposal of fixed asset, removed from suspense account		

Task 10

Valuation of raw materials stock (lower of cost and net realisable value)

	£
Material X	3,417.22
Material Y	4,719.33
Total	8,136.55

Manufacturing account for the year ended 31 March 1998

	£
Raw materials	
Opening stock	6,294.33
Purchases	59,103.11
	65,397.44
Closing stock	(8,136.55)
	57,260.89
Direct labour	66,027.37
Prime cost	123,288.26
Factory overheads	30,492.51
Factory cost of finished goods produced	153,780.77

The cost of 25,613 units is £153,780.77, a unit cost of production of £6.004.

The value of closing stock (3,117 units) is therefore £18,714.47.

SOLUTION TO PRACTICE DEVOLVED ASSESSMENT 1: REGGIE STIR

Tutorial note. When doing the journal entries you should not record the purchase of the potter's wheel. This is because the purchase was for *cash* and the journal only records *credit* purchases. The book of prime entry for cash purchases of fixed assets is the cash book.

Solution

(a)

	JOURNAL			Page 50
Date	Details	Folio Ref	£	£
3 August	Plant and equipment	P/E	1600	
	Plant and equipment disposals	P/D		500
	Cumere Oven Ltd	C/O		1100
	Being part exchange per agreement and invoice no 35X42			
3 August	Plant and equipment: disposals	NP/D	1200	
	Plant and equipment	P/E		1200
	Being transfer of plant (1/K) at cost to plant disposals a/c			
3 August	Plant and equipment: depreciation provision	PD/P	400	
	Plant and equipment: disposal	NP/D		400
	Being transfer of depreciation provision (1/K) to plant disposals a/c			
10 October	Motor vehicles	M/V	9000	
	Motor vehicles disposals	MV/D		1000
	Van Guard Ltd	V/G		8000
	Being part exchange per agreement and invoice no Z/2643			
10 October	Motor vehicles disposals	MV/D	4000	
	Motor vehicles	M/V		4000
	Being transfer of van 1/V at cost to disposals a/c			

JOURNAL

Page 51

Date	Details	Folio Ref	£	£
10 October	Motor vehicles: depreciation provision	MV/DP	3051	
	Motor vehicles: disposals	MV/D		3051
	Being transfer of depreciation provision 1V to motor vehicles disposals a/c			
31 December	P & L a/c	P/L	300	
	Plant and equipment: disposals a/c	P/D		300
	Being loss on part exchange of kiln 1/K			
31 December	Motor vehicles: disposals	MV/D	51	
	P & L a/c	P/L		51
	Being profit on part exchange of van 1/V			
31 December	Plant and equipment: depreciation expense	P/DE	1147	
	Plant and equipment: depreciation provision	PD/P		1147
	Being year end provision for depreciation on plant			
31 December	Motor vehicles depreciation expense	MV/DE	4594	
	Motor vehicles depreciation provision	MV/DP		4594
	Being year end provision for depreciation on motor vehicles			

LEDGER ACCOUNTS

PLANT AND EQUIPMENT

Date		£	Date		£
1995			*1995*		
1 Jan	Balance b/f	4,970	3 Aug	Plant and equipment:	
3 Aug	Creditors £(1,600 – 500)	1,100		disposals	1,200
3 Aug	Plant and equipment:		31 Dec	Balance c/f	5,870
	disposals	500			
5 Sep	Bank	500			
		7,070			7,070

PLANT AND EQUIPMENT: PROVISION FOR DEPRECIATION

Date		£	Date		£
1995			*1995*		
3 Aug	Plant and equipment:		1 Jan	Balance b/f	2,330
	disposals	400	31 Dec	P & L a/c (W1)	1,147
31 Dec	Balance c/f	3,077			
		3,477			3,477

PLANT AND EQUIPMENT: DISPOSALS

Date		£	Date		£
1995			*1995*		
3 Aug	Plant and equipment	1,200	3 Aug	Depreciation provision	400
			3 Aug	Plant and equipment	500
			31 Dec	P & L account	300
		1,200			1,200

MOTOR VEHICLES

Date		£	Date		£
1995			*1995*		
1 Jan	Balance b/f	18,000	10 Oct	Motor vehicles:	
10 Oct	Motor vehicles:			disposals	4,000
	disposals	1,000	31 Dec	Balance c/f	23,000
10 Oct	Creditors £(9,000 – 1,000)	8,000			
		27,000			27,000

MOTOR VEHICLES: PROVISION FOR DEPRECIATION

Date		£	Date		£
1995			*1995*		
10 Oct	Motor vehicles:		1 Jan	Balance b/f	7,676
	disposals	3,051	31 Dec	P & L a/c (W2)	4,594
31 Dec	Balance c/f	9,219			
		12,270			12,270

MOTOR VEHICLES: DISPOSALS

Date		£	Date		£
1995			*1995*		
10 Oct	Motor vehicles	4,000	10 Oct	Depreciation provision	3,051
31 Dec	P & L account	51	10 Oct	Motor vehicles	1,000
		4,051			4,051

PLANT AND EQUIPMENT

Ref	Description	Date of purchase	Cost £	Depreciation period	Accumulated depreciation 31 Dec 1995 £	Date of disposal	Net book value 31 Dec 1995 £	Sale/scrap proceeds £	(Loss)/ profit £
1/K	Kiln	1 Jan 1993	1200	6 years	400	3 Aug 1995	800	500	(300)
1/P	Pugmill	1 July 1994	300	4 years	150		150		
2/K	Kiln	1 Mar 1992	600	6 years	400		200		
3/K	Kiln	20 Aug 1991	750	6 years	625		125		
1/W	Wheel	31 Mar 1993	400	4 years	300		100		
2/W	Wheel	1 Feb 1992	400	4 years	400		nil		
4/K	Kiln	1 Sep 1992	900	6 years	600		300		
3/W	Wheel	1 Mar 1994	420	4 years	210		210		
5/K	Kiln	3 Aug 1995	1600	6 years	267		1333		
4/W	Wheel	5 Sept 1995	500	4 years	125		375		
Totals			7070		3477		3593		
Disposals			1200		400		800	500	(300)
Totals c/f			5870		3077		2793		

MOTOR VEHICLES

Ref	Description	Date of purchase	Cost £	Depreciation type	Accumulated depreciation 31 Dec 1995 £	Date of disposal	Net book value 31 Dec 1995 £	Sale/scrap proceeds £	(Loss)/ profit £
1/V	Van reg D249 NPO	1 Feb 1990	4000	Reducing balance 25%	3051	10 Oct 1995	949	1000	51
2/V	Van reg K697 JKL	1 Jan 1993	6000	Reducing balance 25%	3469		2531		
3/V	Van reg J894 TMG	30 Sept 1994	8000	Reducing balance 25%	3500		4500		
4/V	Van reg N583 MNO	10 Oct 1995	9000	Reducing balance 25%	2250		6750		
Totals			27000		12270		14730		
Disposals			4000		3051		949	1000	51
Totals c/f			23000		9219		13781		

Workings

1   *Depreciation charge: plant and equipment*

	£
Kilns £(600 + 750 + 900 + 1,600) ÷ 6	642
Other £(300 + 400 + 400 + 420 + 500) ÷ 4	505
	1,147

Note. It should be assumed from the question that all kilns are depreciated over 6 years and all wheels over 4 years.

2   *Depreciation charge: motor vehicles*

	£	£
Van 2/V: NBV 1 January 1995	3,375	
Depreciation @ 25%		844
Van 3/V: NBV 1 January 1995	6,000	
Depreciation @ 25%		1,500
Van 4/V: depreciation (25% × £9,000)		2,250
Total charge to P & L		4,594

(b) REGGIE STIR LIMITED
   BALANCE SHEET EXTRACT AS AT 31 DECEMBER 1995

	Cost £	Accumulated depreciation £	NBV £
Fixed assets			
Plant and equipment	5,870	3,077	2,793
Motor vehicles	23,000	9,219	13,781
	28,870	12,296	16,574

SOLUTION TO PRACTICE DEVOLVED ASSESSMENT 2: BOOTHS

Tutorial note. You will realise from your earlier studies that the sales and purchase invoices shown in the question would normally be posted to the sales day book and purchases day book respectively. We have bypassed the day books in the example, for the sake of simplicity and because the main emphasis of the assignment is the posting of transactions to the correct ledger accounts.

Solution

(a) and (b)

The ledger accounts will appear as follows after the postings for 30 June 19X7 and after being balanced off.

ADVERTISING					
19X7			19X7		
29 June Balance b/f	288	91			
30 June Bank	33	50	30 June P+L account	322	41
	322	41		322	41

ACCOUNTANCY FEES					
19X7			19X7		
29 June Balance b/f	1,500	00	30 June P+L account	1,500	00

BANK ACCOUNT					
19X7			19X7		
29 June Balance b/f	19,330	65			
			30 June Woodley Gazette	39	36
			Electricity	739	80
			M Able & Co	1,437	50
			Interest bank	67	48
			Pratts Garage	372	97
			Post Office	378	12
			Halfway Investments	2,312	50
			Wages	2,169	52
30 June Balance c/f	3,729	33	Motor vehicles + road tax	15,542	73
	23,059	98		23,059	98

DOUBTFUL DEBT PROVISION

19X7			19X7		
30 June Balance c/f	1,242	94	29 June Balance b/f	1,242	94

ELECTRICITY

19X7			19X7		
29 June Balance b/f	1,733	84			
30 June Bank	629	62	30 June P+L account	2,363	46
	2,363	46		2,363	46

FIXTURES AND FITTINGS

19X7			19X7		
29 June Balance b/f	11,893	55	30 June Balance c/f	11,893	55

GAS

19X7			19X7		
29 June Balance b/f	1,161	20	30 June P+L account	1,161	20

INSURANCE

19X7			19X7		
29 June Balance b/f	658	38			
30 June Bank	1,437	50	30 June P+L account	2,095	88
	2,095	88		2,095	88

INTEREST

19X7			19X7		
29 June Balance b/f	1,141	31			
30 June Bank	67	48	30 June P+L account	1,208	79
	1,208	79		1,208	79

MAINTENANCE					
19X7			19X7		
29 June Balance b/f	3,807	43	30 June P+L account	3,807	43

MOTOR EXPENSES					
19X7			19X7		
29 June Balance b/f	606	19			
30 June Bank	317	42			
* Bank	100	00			
** Bank	1,437	50	30 June P+L account	2,461	11
	2,461	11		2,461	11

MOTOR VEHICLES					
19X7			19X7		
29 June Balance b/f	43,675	07			
30 June Bank	15,442	73	30 June Balance c/f	59,117	80
	59,117	80		59,117	80

PROFIT AND LOSS ACCOUNT					
19X7			19X7		
30 June Balance c/f	27,225	92	29 June Balance b/f	27,225	92

PURCHASES					
19X7			19X7		
29 June Balance b/f	76,648	31			
30 June Larkin Lumber					
P/L Control a/c	3,295	00			
Plumbing supplies					
P/L Control a/c	1,536	05	30 June P+L account	81,479	36
	81,479	36		81,479	36

* A prepayment would not normally be required for such a small amount; in any case this would not be calculated until the ETB was prepared.

** This amount might have been posted to the insurance account, depending on company policy, but this is more appropriate.

PURCHASE LEDGER CONTROL A/C

19X7			19X7		
			29 June Balance b/f	9,554	93
			30 June Larkin Lumber	3,871	63
30 June Balance c/f	15,231	42	Plumbing supplies	1,804	86
	15,231	42		15,231	42

PRINT, POSTAGE & STATIONERY

19X7			19X7		
29 June Balance b/f	117	29			
30 June Bank	378	12	30 June P+L account	495	41
	495	41		495	41

RENT

19X7			19X7		
29 June Balance b/f	9,250	00			
30 June Bank	2,312	50	30 June P+L account	11,562	50
	11,562	50		11,562	50

Note. The rent invoice just paid is for rent to 30 September 19X7. This would be adjusted as a prepayment on the *extended* trial balance.

SHARE CAPITAL

19X7			19X7		
30 June Balance c/f	10,000	00	29 June Balance b/f	10,000	00

ACCUMULATED DEPRECIATION

19X7			19X7		
30 June Balance c/f	27,241	12	29 June Balance b/f	27,241	12

SALES					
19X7			19X7		
			29 June Balance b/f	180,754	17
			30 June Sales Ledger		
			Control a/c		
			MP Price & Co	504	00
			H Contractors	90	45
			NP Plumbers	342	75
30 June Balance c/f	182,421	37	CR Harris & Co	730	00
	182,421	37		182,421	37

SALES LEDGER CONTROL A/C					
19X7			19X7		
29 June Balance b/f	19,356	30			
30 June Sales					
MP Price & Co	592	20			
H Contractors	106	28			
NP PLumbers	402	73			
CR Harris & Co	857	75	30 June Balance c/f	21,315	26
	21,315	26		21,315	26

SUNDRY EXPENSES					
19X7,			19X7		
29 June Balance b/f	1,427	70	30 June P+L account	1,427	70

OPENING STOCK					
19X7			19X7		
29 June Balance b/f	37,321	56	30 June Balance c/f	37,321	56

TELEPHONE					
19X7			19X7		
29 June Balance b/f	3,879	09	30 June P & L account	3,879	09

UNIFORM BUSINESS RATE					
19X7			19X7		
29 June Balance b/f	4,917	94	30 June P & L account	4,917	94

VAT CONTROL A/C					
19X7			19X7		
30 June Bank	5	86	29 June Balance b/f	6,719	19
Bank	110	18	30 June Sales ledger	88	20
Bank	55	55	Sales ledger	15	83
Purchases ledger	576	63	Sales ledger	59	98
Purchases ledger	268	81	Sales ledger	127	75
Balance c/f	5,993	92			
	7,010	95		7,010	95

WAGES					
19X7			19X7		
29 June Balance b/f	21,575	63			
30 June Bank	2,169	52	30 June P & L account	23,745	15
	23,745	15		23,745	15

WATER RATES					
19X7			19X7		
29 June Balance b/f	2,447	92	30 June P & L account	2,447	92

(c)   The balances on the ledger accounts, once extracted, will give the following trial balance.

FOLIO	DESCRIPTION	REF.	TRIAL BALANCE			
	Advertising		322	41		
	Accountancy fees		1,500	00		
	Bank				3,729	33
	Depreciation (accumulated)				27,241	12
	Doubtful debt provision				1,242	94
	Electricity		2,363	46		
	Fixtures and fittings		11,893	55		
	Gas		1,161	20		
	Insurance		658	38		
	Interest		1,208	79		
	Maintenance		3,807	43		
	Motor expenses		2,461	11		
	Motor vehicles		59,117	80		
	Profit and loss account				27,225	92
	Purchases		81,479	36		
	Purchase ledger control a/c				15,231	42
	Print, post and stationery		495	41		
	Rent		11,562	50		
	Share capital				10,000	00
	Sales				182,421	37
	Sales ledger control a/c		21,315	26		
	Sundry expenses		1,427	70		
	Stock 1.1 X4		37,321	56		
	Telephone		3,879	09		
	Unified Business Rate		4,917	94		
	VAT				5,993	92
	Wages		23,745	15		
	Water rates		2,447	92		
	TOTAL		273,086	02	273,086	02

(d)   The following accruals and prepayments should be identified.

Accruals

Franking services: £378.12 × 1/3 = £126.04

Prepayments

Rent: quarter to 30 September 19X7: £2,312.50

Motor insurance: £1,437.50 × 11/12 = £1,317.71

SOLUTION TO PRACTICE DEVOLVED ASSESSMENT 3: LAKELAND CATERING

Shop and restaurant

Task (a)

Statement of affairs as at 1 January 1996

	£	£
Assets		
Vehicle	5,800	
Restaurant fittings	3,900	
Stock	6,000	
Debtors	200	
Bank	350	
Prepayment	150	
		16,400
Less: liabilities		
Creditors	(1,100)	
Accruals - rent	(250)	
- wages	(610)	
		(1,960)
Capital (as at 1 January 1996)		14,440

Task (b)

Closing cash position as at 31 December 1996

	£	£
Receipts		
Opening balance	350	
Sales	31,970	
		32,320
Payments		(28,917)
Closing cash book balance		3,403

Task (c)

Control accounts

Trade debtors

	£		£
b/f 1 January 1996	200	Cash/bank	4,910
P&L	5,325	c/f 31 December 1996	615
	5,525		5,525
b/f 1 January 1997	615		

Trade creditors

	£		£
Cash/bank	17,850	b/f 1 January 1996	1,100
c/f 31 December 1996	840	P&L	17,590
	18,690		18,690
		b/f 1 January 1997	840

Rent

	£		£
Cash/bank	745	b/f 1 January 1996	250
		P&L	435
		c/f 31 December 1996	60
	745		745
b/f 1 January 1997	60		

Wages

	£		£
Cash/bank	8,090	b/f 1 January 1996	610
		P&L	7,480
	8,090		8,090

Electricity

	£		£
b/f 1 January 1996	150	P&L	1,040
Cash/bank	640		
c/f 31 December 1996	250		
	1,040		1,040
		b/f 1 January 1997	250

Task (d)

Shop and restaurant

Trading and profit and loss account for the period ended 31 December 1996

		£	£
Sales			32,385
Opening stock		6,000	
Add: purchases		17,590	
		23,590	
Less: closing stock		(5,400)	
Cost of goods sold			(18,190)
Gross profit			14,195
Less: rent		435	
wages		7,480	
electricity		1,040	
depreciation	- fittings	780	
	- vehicle	1,740	
telephone		570	
restaurant maintenance		710	
insurance		312	
			(13,067)
Net profit			1,128

Task (e)

Shop and restaurant

Balance sheet as at 31 December 1996

	b/f £	Depn £	NBV £
Fixed assets			
Fittings	3,900	(780)	3,120
Van	5,800	(1,740)	4,060
	9,700	(2,520)	7,180
Current assets			
Stock	5,400		
Debtors	615		
Rent prepayment	60		
Cash	3,403		
		9,478	
Less: current liabilities			
Creditors	840		
Accrual - electricity	250		
		(1,090)	
			8,388
			15,568
Financed by			
Capital as at 1 January 1996			14,440
Net profit			1,128
			15,568

Task (f)

MEMORANDUM

To: David
From: Caroline
Date: 31 January 1997

Depreciation methods

Straight line depreciation is obtained by calculating a fixed annual sum by which an asset will be depreciated. So, for example, if an asset was purchased for £10,000 and is to be depreciated over four years and have an expected selling price at the end of four years of £4,100 then the annual depreciation charge per annum will be £1,475.

The reducing balance method of depreciation means that the depreciation charged against profits reduces year on year. The main justification for using this method is that each year, as the machine wears out, more and more will be spent on repairing and maintaining it. The reducing balance method is expressed as a percentage of the book value so, for example, if we use a reducing balance percentage of 20% for the previous example the figures would be as follows.

Cost £10,000

	Calculation	*Depreciation*	*Book value*
End of year			
1	£10,000 × 20%	£2,000	£8,000
2	£8,000 × 20%	£1,600	£6,400
etc.			

Task (g)

Van depreciation - straight line method

$$\text{Depreciation charge} = \frac{10,000 - 460}{6} = 1,590$$

		Depreciation charge for year £	Book value £
End of year	1	1,590	8,410
	2	1,590	6,820
	3	1,590	5,230
	4	1,590	3,640
	5	1,590	2,050
	6	1,590	460

Task (h)

Van depreciation - reducing balance method

Cost = £10,000

		Calculation of depreciation charge £	Depreciation charge for year £	Book value £
End of year	1	10,000 × 40%	4,000	6,000
	2	6,000 × 40%	2,400	3,600
	3	3,600 × 40%	1,440	2,160
	4	2,160 × 40%	864	1,296
	5	1,296 × 40%	518	778
	6	778 × 40%	311	467

For task (i)

LAKELAND CATERING - SPECIALIST CATERING DIVISION

Description	Trial balance Debit £	Trial balance Credit £	Adjustments Debit £	Adjustments Credit £	Accruals £	Pre-payments £	Profit and loss account Debit £	Profit and loss account Credit £	Balance sheet Debit £	Balance sheet Credit £
Sales		38,500						38,500		
Purchases	19,250						19,250			
Opening stock	4,000						4,000			
Wages	10,100						10,100			
Electricity	750				100		850			
P/L Depn -fittings			250				250			
-vehicles			1,590				1,590			
Telephone	600		50				650			
Insurance	450			50			400			
Rent	950					250	700			
Fixtures - cost	5,000								5,000	
depn		2,500		250						2,750
Vehicle - cost	10,000								10,000	
depn				1,590						1,590
Stock - bal sheet			3,000						3,000	
trading a/c				3,000				3,000		
Debtors	700								700	
Creditors		1,200								1,200
Cash in hand	100								100	
Bank over-draft		1,400								1,400
Capital		8,300								8,300
Prepayments									250	
Accruals										100
Net profit							3,710			3,710
TOTALS	51,900	51,900	4,890	4,890	100	250	41,500	41,500	19,050	19,050

SOLUTION TO PRACTICE DEVOLVED ASSESSMENT 4: CUT PRICE ELECTRICALS

Task (a)

Cut Price Electricals retail division opening capital statement as at 1 November 1995

	DR £'000	CR £'000
Premises - cost	100	
Premises - depreciation		20
Fixtures - cost	85	
Fixtures - depreciation		15
Vans - cost	20	
Vans - depreciation		10
Stock	36	
Debtors	20	
Creditors		16
Wages - in advance	2	
Rent - in advance	7	
Rates - in arrears		6
Advertising - in arrears		5
Insurance - in advance	6	
Cash in hand	2	
Bank overdraft		7
Capital as at 1/11/95 (balancing item)		199
	278	278

Task (b)

Control accounts - Retail Division

Wages

	£'000		£'000
b/f 1/11/95	2	P&L	76
Cash/bank	79	c/f 31/10/96	5
	81		81
b/f 1/11/96	5		

Rent

	£'000		£'000
b/f 1/11/95	7	P&L	21
Cash/bank	17	c/f 31/10/96	3
	24		24
b/f 1/11/96	3		

Rates

	£'000		£'000
Cash/bank	14	b/f 1/11/95	6
c/f 31/10/96	2	P&L	10
	16		16
		b/f 1/11/96	2

Advertising

	£'000		£'000
Cash/bank	8	b/f 1/11/95	5
c/f 31/10/96	8	P&L	11
	16		16
		b/f 1/11/96	8

Insurance

	£'000		£'000
b/f 1/11/95	6	P&L	25
Cash/bank	16		
c/f 31/10/96	3		
	25		25
		b/f 1/11/96	3

Trade debtors

	£'000		£'000
b/f 1/11/95	20	Cash/bank	212
P&L	206	c/f 31/10/96	14
	226		226
b/f 1/11/96	14		

Trade creditors

	£'000		£'000
Cash/bank	104	b/f 1/11/95	16
c/f 31/10/96	27	P&L	115
	131		131
		b/f 1/11/96	27

Task (c)

Cut Price Electricals
Bank Reconciliation Statement

	£
Balance as per bank statement	(44,350)
Unlodged credits	17,000
Uncleared cheques	(2,650)
Balance as per cash book	(30,000)

Tasks (d) and (e)

Fixed asset register as at 31 October 1996
Van number 2

Cost	Depreciation to 31/10/95	Depreciation for year ended 31/10/96	Net book value at 31/10/96
£10,000	£4,000	£2,000	£4,000

Van number 1

Van account

	£'000		£'000
b/f 1/11/95	<u>10</u>	Asset disposal	<u>10</u>

Van depreciation account

	£'000		£'000
Asset disposal	8	b/f 1/11/95	6
	<u>8</u>	Charge for year	<u>2</u> 8

Asset disposal account

	£'000		£'000
Van	10.0	Depreciation account	8.0
Profit on disposal to P&L	<u>1.5</u>	Cash/bank	<u>3.5</u>
	11.5		11.5

Tasks (f), (g), (h)

CUT PRICE ELECTRICALS - INSTALLATION AND CONTRACTING DIVISION

Description	Trial balance Debit £'000	Trial balance Credit £'000	Adjustments Debit £'000	Adjustments Credit £'000	Accruals £'000	Pre-payments £'000	Profit and loss account Debit £'000	Profit and loss account Credit £'000	Balance sheet Debit £'000	Balance sheet Credit £'000
Sales		109						109		
Purchases	64						64			
Stock	11						11			
Wages	57						57			
Van expenses	14			3			11			
Travel expenses	3		3				6			
Garage rent	6					1	5			
Insurance	2						2			
Tools allowance	5						5			
Advertising	8				2		10			
Misc - expenses	4						4			
Vans - cost	20								20	
Vans - depn		12		6						18
Fixtures - cost	75								75	
Fixtures - depn		60		3						63
Capital		100								100
Debtors	36								36	
Creditors		21								21
Cash in hand	6								6	
Bank overdraft		9								9
Stock - B sheet			14						14	
- Trading a/c				14				14		
P/L Depn - Vans			6				6			
- Fixtures			3				3			
Bad debt provsn - B sheet				2						2
- P/L a/c			2				2			
Prepayments/accruals					2	1			1	2
Net loss								63	63	
	311	311	28	28	2	1	186	186	215	215

SOLUTIONS TO TRIAL RUN
DEVOLVED ASSESSMENT

	PLANT AND EQUIPMENT								
Ref	Description	Date of purchase	Cost £	Depreciation period	Accumulated depreciation 31.12.X6 £	Date of disposal	Net book value 31.12.X6 £	Sale/scrap proceeds £	(Loss)/ profit £
P111	Cutter	1.3.X2	24,750	5 years	24,750		- - - - -		
P112	Moulding machine	2.5.X3	12,300	6 years	8,200		4,100		
P113	Assembler	6.6.X3	18,280	4 years	18,280		- - - - -		
Totals			55,330		51,230		4,100		

	MOTOR VEHICLES								
Ref	Description	Date of purchase	Cost £	Depreciation type	Accumulated depreciation 31.12.X6 £	Date of disposal	Net book value 31.12.X6 £	Sale/scrap proceeds £	(Loss)/ profit £
M111	Van reg F396 HJB	22.2.X2	6,500	Reducing balance 25%	4,444	3.8.X6	2,056	2,000	56
M112	Van reg H842 GSL	17.3.X4	8,500	Reducing balance 25%	4,914		3,586		
M113	Van reg J542 KLH	12.9.X5	10,500	Reducing balance 25%	4,594		5,906		
M114	Van reg K125 ATE	3.8.X6	12,000	Reducing balance 25%	3,000		9,000		
Totals			37,500		16,952		20,548		
Disposals			6,500		4,444		2,056	2,000	56
Totals c/f			31,000		12,508		18,492		

	LEASEHOLD PREMISES								
Ref	Description	Date of purchase	Cost £	Term of lease	Accumulated amortisation 31.12.X6 £	Date of disposal	Net book value 31.12.X6 £	Disposal proceeds £	(Loss)/ profit £
L110	Leasehold property	1.1.X2	100,000	50 years	10,000		90,000		

LEDGER ACCOUNTS

MOTOR VEHICLES

		£			£
Date			*Date*		
19X6			*19X6*		
1 Jan	Balance b/d	25,500	3 Aug	Motor vehicles:	
3 Aug	Motor vehicles: disposals	2,000		disposals	6,500
3 Aug	Sundry creditors	10,000	31 Dec	Balance c/d	31,000
		37,500			37,500

MOTOR VEHICLES: PROVISION FOR DEPRECIATION

		£			£
Date			*Date*		
19X6			*19X6*		
3 Aug	Motor vehicles: disposals	4,444	1 Jan	Balance b/d	10,788
31 Dec	Balance c/d	12,508	31 Dec	Motor vehicles:	
				depreciation (W1)	6,164
		16,952			16,952

MOTOR VEHICLES: DISPOSALS

		£			£
Date			*Date*		
19X6			*19X6*		
3 Aug	Motor vehicles	6,500	3 Aug	Motor vehicles	2,000
			3 Aug	Provision for	
				depreciation	4,444
			31 Dec	Profit and loss	56
		6,500			6,500

	JOURNAL			Page 20
Date	Details	Folio Ref	£	£
3 August	Motor vehicles	M110	12,000	
	Motor vehicles disposals	M150		2,000
	Sundry creditors	L300		10,000
	Being purchase of van K125 ATE by part exchange			
3 August	Motor vehicles disposals	M150	6,500	
	Motor vehicles	M110		6,500
	Being transfer of van F396 HJB at cost to disposals a/c			
3 August	Motor vehicles depreciation provision	M120	4,444	
	Motor vehicles disposals	M150		4,444
	Being transfer of depreciation provision to motor vehicles a/c Profit and loss a/c			
31 December	Profit and loss a/c	P200	56	
	Motor vehicles disposals a/c	M150		56
	Being loss on part exchange of van F306 HJB			
31 December	Motor vehicles depreciation	M130(W1)	6,164	
	Motor vehicles depreciation provision	M120		6,164
	Being year end provision for depreciation on motor vehicles			
31 December	Plant and equipment depreciation	P130(W3)	11,570	
	Plant and equipment depreciation provision	P120		11,570
	Being year end provision for depreciation on plant and equipment			

	JOURNAL			Page 21
Date	Details	Folio Ref	£	£
	Leasehold premises amortisation	L130(W2)	2,000	
	Leasehold premises accumluated amortisation	L120		2,000
	Being year end amortisation on leasehold premises			
31 December	Repairs and maintenance	R200	4,770	
	Suspense a/c	S400		4,770
	Being elimination of suspense a/c balance and correct classification of expense			
31 December	Bad debt expense a/c	B200	200	
	Trade debtors	D100		200
	Being bad debt written off			
31 December	Bad debt expense a/c	B200	2,354	
	Bad debt provision	B100		2,354
	Being bad debt provision			

Folio	Account	Trial balance Debit £	Trial balance Credit £	Adjustments Debit £	Adjustments Credit £	Accrued £	Prepaid £	Profit and loss a/c Debit £	Profit and loss a/c Credit £	Balance sheet Debit £	Balance sheet Credit £
P110	Plant & equipment: cost	55,330								55,330	
P120	Plant & equipment: dep'n provision		51,230								51,230
P130	Plant & equipment: dep'n expense	11,570						11,570			
M110	Motor vehicles: cost	31,000								31,000	
M120	Motor vehicles: dep'n provision		12,508								12,508
M130	Motor vehicles: dep'n expense	6,164						6,164			
L110	Leasehold premises: cost	100,000								100,000	
L120	Leasehold premises: acc amortis'n		10,000								10,000
L130	Leasehold premises: amortis'n exp	2,000						2,000			
C300	Sundry creditors		13,500								13,500
F100	Bank	6,132								6,132	
F200	Cash in hand	505								505	
A100	Accountancy fee	600				1,500		2,100			
B100	Bad debts provision		150		2,354						2,504
B200	Bad debt expense			2,554				2,554			
L300	Loan		10,000								10,000
R200	Repairs and maintenance	813		4,770				5,583			
M300	Motor expenses	1,506						1,506			
S100	Sales		205,806						205,806		
D100	Trade debtors	50,287			200					50,087	
P100	Purchases	158,142						158,142			
C100	Trade creditors		65,416								65,416
E100	Electricity	900				200		1,100			
P300	Printing, postage, stationery	3,717						3,717			
P200	Profit and loss account		40,956								40,956
S200	Stock at 1.1.X6	9,125						9,125			
S300	Share capital		100,000								100,000
S400	Suspense account	4,770			4,770						
S500	Sundry expenses	6,428						6,428			
W100	Wages and salaries	60,521					600	59,921			
M400	Loss on sale of van	56						56			
S200P	Stock at 31.12.X6 (B/S)			10,412						10,412	
S200B	Stock at 31.12.X6 (P&L)				10,412				10,412		
	Prepayments/accruals					1,700	600			600	1,700
	SUB-TOTAL	509,566	509,566	17,736	17,736	1,700	600	269,966	216,218	254,066	307,814
	Profit for the year								53,748	53,748	
	TOTAL	509,566	509,566	17,736	17,736	1,700	600	269,966	269,966	307,814	307,814

Workings

1   *Depreciation expense: motor vehicles*

Ref		£
M112	£4,781 × 25%	1,195
M113	£7,875 × 25%	1,969
M114	£12,000 × 25%	3,000
	Total	6,164

2   *Depreciation expense: premises*

$$\frac{£100,000}{50} = £2,000$$

3   *Depreciation expense: plant and equipment*

Ref		£
P111	£24,750 ÷ 5	4,950
P112	£12,300 ÷ 6	2,050
P113	£18,280 ÷ 4	4,570
		11,570

4   *Bad debts provision*

	£
Trade debtors per trial balance	50,287
Less bad debt written off	200
	50,087
Provision required (£50,087 × 5%)	2,504
Provision b/d	150
Increase required	2,354

Total bad debt expense £(200 + 2,354) = £2,554

Unit 5
Cost Information

SAMPLE SIMULATION

INTERMEDIATE STAGE - NVQ/SVQ3

Unit 5

Recording cost information
(AAT Sample)

This Sample Simulation is the AAT's Sample Simulation for Unit 5. Its purpose is to give you an idea of what an AAT simulation looks like. It is not intended as a definitive guide to the tasks you may be required to perform.

The suggested time allowance for this Assessment is four hours. Up to 30 minutes extra time may be permitted in an AAT simulation. Breaks in assessment may be allowed in the AAT simulation, but it must normally be completed in one day.

Calculators may be used but no reference material is permitted.

**DO NOT OPEN THIS PAPER UNTIL YOU ARE READY TO START
UNDER TIMED CONDITIONS**

INSTRUCTIONS

This Simulation is designed to test your ability to record cost information.

Background information is provided on Page 159.

The tasks you are to perform are set out on Pages 160 to 161.

You are provided with data on Pages 162 to 171 which you must use to complete the tasks.

Your answers should be set out in the answer booklet on Pages 173 to 188 using the documents provided. You may require additional answer pages.

You are allowed **four hours** to complete your work.

A high level of accuracy is required. Check your work carefully.

Correcting fluid may not be used. Errors should be crossed out neatly and clearly. You should write in black ink, not pencil.

You are advised to read the whole of the Simulation before commencing as all of the information may be of value and is not necessarily supplied in the sequence in which you might wish to deal with it.

A full suggested solution to this Simulation is provided in this Kit on Pages 279 to 294.

THE SITUATION

Introduction

Your name is Lesley Hunt and you work as an accounts assistant for Polycot Ltd, a manufacturer of cotton duvet covers.

Cost centres

The production cost centres in Polycot Ltd are a cutting department, a finishing department and a packing department.

- Work in the cutting department is machine-intensive. The machines are operated by a number of direct employees.

- Work in the finishing department and packing department is labour-intensive, and is carried out entirely by direct employees of Polycot Ltd.

In addition to the production cost centres there is also a stores department.

Cost accounting records

Polycot Ltd uses the FIFO method for valuing issues of materials to production and stocks of materials.

The company is registered for VAT and all of its outputs are standard-rated. This means that VAT on its purchases can always be reclaimed and should therefore be ignored in the cost records.

The accounts code list for the company includes the following codes:

Cost centre codes		*Expenditure codes*	
C100	Cutting department	E200	Direct materials
C200	Finishing department	E210	Indirect materials
C300	Packing department	E300	Direct wages
C400	Stores	E310	Indirect wages
		E410	Indirect revenue expenses
		E500	Depreciation - production equipment

Until now, the company has absorbed all production overheads on the basis of a percentage of direct labour costs. However, as you will see, a change is proposed in this area for the coming year. Whatever method of overhead absorption is used, any under or over absorption is transferred to the profit and loss account at the end of each quarter.

Personnel

The personnel involved in the simulation are as follows:

Production manager	Jim Stubbs
General manager	Patrick McGrath

In the simulation you will begin by dealing with certain transactions in the month of March 1998, and you will then be involved in forecasting outcomes for the company's financial year ending 31 March 1999. Finally, you will use your results to account for transactions in July 1998. Note that for many of the tasks you will need to prepare rough workings; you should use the paper provided for this purpose on Page 188 of the answer booklet.

TASKS TO BE COMPLETED

Part 1: Transactions in March 1998

1   Refer to the invoices and materials requisitions on Pages 162 - 166. Using this information you are required to complete the stores ledger accounts on Pages 175 and 176 of the answer booklet for the month of March 1998. You are reminded that the company uses the FIFO method. You may assume that suppliers raise invoices on the same day as goods are delivered.

2   You are required to prepare a memo for the general manager, Patrick McGrath, drawing attention to any unusual matters concerning stock levels of the items dealt with in task 1 above. Use the blank memo form on Page 177 of the answer booklet and date your memo 3 April 1998.

3   Timesheets for two employees of Polycot Ltd are shown on Pages 178 and 179 of the answer booklet. These employees work on production of duvet covers. Using the information contained in the internal policy document on Page 167 of this booklet, you are required to analyse their wages for the week ending 6 March 1998, as follows:

   •   Complete the total column in each timesheet.

   •   Check for discrepancies and make any necessary adjustments.

   •   Calculate the bonus earned by each employee on each day and in total for the week, and enter the appropriate amounts on the timesheets.

   •   Complete the analysis at the bottom of each timesheet.

   •   Enter the appropriate figures on the cost ledger data entry sheet on Page 180 of the answer booklet.

4   Prepare a memo to the production manager, Jim Stubbs, outlining any discrepancies in the wages data for these two employees for the week and requesting assistance in resolving your queries. Use the blank memo form on Page 181 of the answer booklet and date your memo 10 March 1998.

Part 2: Overhead absorption for 1998/99

5   The company at present absorbs all production overheads as a percentage of direct labour costs. The company is considering a revision in this policy for the accounting year 1998/99. Under the proposed new policy, a machine hour rate would be used in the cutting department, and direct labour hour rates in the finishing and packing departments. You are required to write a memo to the production manager, Jim Stubbs, explaining why this proposal is appropriate. Use the blank memo form on Page 182 of the answer booklet and date your memo 10 March 1998.

6   Refer to the information given on Page 168. Using this information, you are required to calculate 1998/99 overhead absorption rates for each production department: cutting (machine hour rate), finishing (direct labour hour rate) and packing (direct labour hour rate). Use the analysis sheet on Page 183 of the answer booklet.

7   Refer to the memo on Page 169. You are required to use the information in this memo to perform the following tasks:

   (a)   Write a memo to the production manager, Jim Stubbs, concerning the query on the wages for the temporary employee. Explain precisely and clearly what information you would need to be able to fully analyse and classify the hours worked by the employee and the wages paid. Use the blank memo form on Page 184 of the answer booklet and date your memo 6 July 1998.

For the remainder of this task, you are required to ignore the pending query concerning the temporary employee.

   (b)   Using the overhead absorption rate that you calculated in task 6 and the information contained in the labour hours analysis, calculate the production overhead absorbed in the packing department during the quarter ending 30 June 1998. Insert your result in the working sheet on Page 185 of the answer booklet.

(c) Using the information on the costs charged to cost centre code C300, determine the total actual production overhead cost for the packing department for the quarter ending 30 June 1998. Insert your result in the working sheet on Page 185 of the answer booklet.

(d) Determine the amount to be transferred to the profit and loss account for the quarter ending 30 June 1998, in respect of under or over absorbed production overheads for the packing department. Indicate clearly whether the overheads are under or over absorbed for the quarter.

Part 3: Standard costs and variances, July 1998

8 Refer to the information on Page 170. Using this information you are required to complete the standard cost card on Page 186 of the answer booklet. Note that you may need to refer to the following information: your completed stores ledger accounts on Pages 175 and 176 of the answer booklet; the direct labour hour rates on Page 167; and the overhead absorption rates that you calculated in task 6.

9 Refer to the memo on Page 171. You are required to prepare a memo, addressed to the general manager, Patrick McGrath, analysing all of the variances arising during the week ended 8 July 1998 in the cutting department and suggesting possible reasons for the main variances. You should date your report 13 July 1998. Use the memo form on Page 187 of the answer booklet.

Note. In addition to the information referred to above, you will also need to refer to the overhead absorption rates that you calculated in task 6 and the standard cost card that you prepared in task 8.

SALES INVOICE

Kenilworth Limited
12 Luton Road, Mapleton, Bedfordshire LU4 8EN
Telephone: 01582 622411

VAT registration: 291 8753 42

Date/tax point: 2 March 1998

Invoice to:
Polycot Limited
17 Hightown Road
Branston BN4 3EW

Invoice number: 2078

Your order: 3901

Item description	Quantity	Unit price £	Trade discount @ 30% £	Net price £	Total £
Plastic poppers (100 in each box)	100 boxes	91.00	27.30	63.70	6,370.00
Total					6,370.00
VAT @ 17.5%					1,114.75
Total due					7,484.75

Terms: net 30 days

SALES INVOICE

Baxter Limited
39 Langdale Avenue, Bisham MW3 9TY
Telephone: 01693 77612

VAT registration: 215 8761 34

Date/tax point: 6 March 1998

Invoice to:
Polycot Limited
17 Hightown Road
Branston BN4 3EW

Invoice number: 7123

Your order: 3889

Item description	Quantity £	Unit price £	Trade discount @ 30% £	Net price £	Total £
Cotton - 50 metre rolls	90	124.00	37.20	86.80	7,812.00
Total					7,812.00
VAT @ 17.5%					1,367.10
Total due					9,179.10

Terms: net 30 days

SALES INVOICE

Kenilworth Limited
12 Luton Road, Mapleton, Bedfordshire LU4
8EN
Telephone: 01582 622411

VAT registration: 291 8753 42

Date/tax point: 9 March 1998

Invoice to:
Polycot Limited
17 Hightown Road
Branston BN4 3EW

Invoice number: 2115

Your order: 3912

Item description	Quantity £	Unit price £	Trade discount @ 30% £	Net price £	Total £
Plastic poppers (100 in each box)	100 boxes	91.00	27.60	64.40	6,440.00
Total VAT @ 17.5%					6,440.00 1,127.00
Total due					7,567.00
Terms: net 30 days					

SALES INVOICE

Hartston Limited
55 Parlour Street, Jamestown, FE6 8UR
Telephone: 01225 67124

VAT registration: 214 5143 28

Date/tax point: 12 March 1998

Invoice to:
Polycot Limited
17 Hightown Road
Branston BN4 3EW

Invoice number: 34415

Your order: 3932

Item description	Quantity £	Unit price £	Trade discount @ 30% £	Net price £	Total £
Plastic poppers (100 in each box)	100 boxes	95.00	28.50	66.50	6,650.00
Total VAT @ 17.5%					6,650.00 1,163.75
Total due					7,813.75
Terms: net 30 days					

SALES INVOICE

Baxter Limited
39 Langdale Avenue, Bisham MW3 9TY
Telephone: 01693 77612

VAT registration: 215 8761 34

Date/tax point: 12 March 1998

Invoice to:
Polycot Limited
17 Hightown Road
Branston BN4 3EW

Invoice number: 7249

Your order: 3917

Item description	Quantity £	Unit price £	Trade discount @ 30% £	Net price £	Total £
Cotton - 50 metre rolls	90	126.00	37.80	88.20	7,938.00

Total		7,938.00
VAT @ 17.5%		1,389.15
Total due		9,327.15

Terms: net 30 days

MATERIALS REQUISITION

DATE *6 March 1998*   NUMBER   *944*

DEPARTMENT   *Finishing*

QUANTITY	CODE	DESCRIPTION
90	PP29	Plastic poppers

SIGNATURE   *Jim Stubbs*

MATERIALS REQUISITION

DATE *10 March 1998*   NUMBER   *948*

DEPARTMENT   *Cutting*

QUANTITY	CODE	DESCRIPTION
50	C733	Cotton, 50 metre rolls

SIGNATURE   *Jim Stubbs*

MATERIALS REQUISITION

DATE *18 March 1998*   NUMBER   *959*

DEPARTMENT   *Cutting*

QUANTITY	CODE	DESCRIPTION
40	C733	Cotton, 50 metre rolls

SIGNATURE   *Jim Stubbs*

MATERIALS REQUISITION

DATE *20 March 1998*   NUMBER   *961*

DEPARTMENT   *Finishing*

QUANTITY	CODE	DESCRIPTION
110	*PP29*	*Plastic poppers*

SIGNATURE   *Jim Stubbs*

MATERIALS REQUISITION

DATE *30 March 1998*   NUMBER   *984*

DEPARTMENT   *Cutting*

QUANTITY	CODE	DESCRIPTION
30	*C733*	*Cotton, 50 metre rolls*

SIGNATURE   *Jim Stubbs*

INTERNAL POLICY DOCUMENT

Document no.   15
Subject: Wages
Issued: December 1997

Direct labour rates to be paid

Employee grade	£ per hour
1	4.00
2	3.00
3	2.50

The above rates are also payable for any hours spent on indirect work.

Direct employees work an eight hour day.

Overtime (any hours worked in excess of eight per day): employees are to be paid for one and a half hours for every hour of overtime that they work.

Employees will be paid a bonus of £0.15 for every duvet cover produced in excess of 60 in any single day. No in lieu bonuses are paid for idle time, training etc.

Employees are to be credited with eight hours for any full days when they are sick, on holiday, or engaged in training activities. Half or part days are credited on a pro rata basis. These hours are to be paid at the basic rate.

Analysis of wages

The following are to be treated as direct labour costs:

*   Payment for hours spent on direct tasks
*   The basic pay for overtime spent on direct tasks

The following are to be treated as indirect labour costs:

*   Overtime premium payments
*   Bonus payments
*   Idle time payments
*   Holiday pay, sick pay and training pay

Discrepancies on time sheets

The company wishes to facilitate the prompt payment of wages and early reporting of labour costs to management. Employees will initially be paid for the total number of hours shown at the bottom of their time sheet, plus appropriate bonuses and overtime premiums.

Any discrepancies on time sheets are to be temporarily adjusted within direct labour hours, pending the outcome of enquiries.

Unit 5: Cost Information

Production overheads for the year to 31 March 1999

Polycot Ltd rents its production premises. The rent and rates for the year to 31 March 1999 will amount to £79,500.

Catering facilities for production staff are limited to a number of vending machines dispensing drinks and snacks. The rent for these machines during the year ending 31 March 1999 will be £100 per month.

Machinery and equipment owned by Polycot is subject to a maintenance contract covering preventive and urgent maintenance, parts, labour and call out charges. For the year to 31 March 1999 the maintenance company will charge £25,250 in respect of the machinery in the cutting department, £5,600 in respect of machinery in the finishing department, £11,000 in respect of machinery in the packing department and £4,000 in respect of machinery in the stores department. Depreciation on all machinery will total £13,490.

The production manager's salary will be £21,000 for the year; he divides his time about equally between the three production departments. The storekeeper's salary will be £14,000.

Other production overheads for the year are estimated at £40,000. The general manager has suggested that this should be divided evenly across the four departments.

The following data is also available.

	Cutting	Finishing	Packing	Stores
Floor area (sq metres)	1,900	2,650	1,900	1,125
Number of employees	20	68	40	3
Cost of machinery	£74,125	£16,625	£32,300	£11,850
Direct labour hours	5,125	129,750	67,500	
Machine hours	30,750	28,350	10,750	
Number of materials requisitions	21,175	17,675	14,100	

MEMO

To: Lesley Hunt
From: Patrick McGrath, General Manager
Date: 3 July 1998
Subject: Overhead absorption, quarter ending 30 June 1998

Your colleague in the accounts department had almost completed the task of calculating the production overheads under or over absorbed for the last quarter. Unfortunately she was not able to complete the task before leaving for her summer holiday. She has asked me to pass on the following information, and assures me that you will know what to do in order to complete the calculations.

Thanks for your help.

Information attached to the memo:

Amounts charged to cost centre code C300 - Packing department: quarter ending 30 June 1998

Cost centre code	Expenditure code	Amount charged £
C300	E200	8,020
C300	E210	855
C300	E300	48,345
C300	E310	4,045
C300	E410	10,800
C300	E500	800

Labour hours analysis - quarter ending 30 June 1998

	Cutting department hours	Finishing department hours	Packing department hours
Direct labour hours	1,200	38,800	18,300
Indirect labour hours	890	1,250	1,830
Total labour hours	2,090	40,050	20,130

Note. The above tables do not include a payment that I still have to enquire about, as follows.

• Wages paid to temporary employee for 320 hours worked during the quarter ending 30 June 1998: £1,920.

Standard costs for 1998/99

The general manager, Patrick McGrath, has informed you of the following decisions relating to standard costs for double duvet covers for the year ending 31 March 1999.

Cotton prices
Assume a 5 per cent increase over the highest price paid in March 1998. (Refer back to the relevant stores ledger card for this information.)

Plastic poppers
Assume a price of £67 per box of 100.

Thread
Assume a price of £14.20 per 10,000 metres.

Packing cartons
Assume a price of £0.25 per box, each box being large enough for 6 double covers.

Direct labour
Assume a 5 per cent increase over current rates for all grades.

MEMO

To: Lesley Hunt
From: Patrick McGrath
Date: 12 July 1998
Subject: Standard cost report for double duvet covers in Cutting department

I have collated some of the data you will need for the standard cost report for week ended 8 July - see below.

Please could you let me have an analysis of all the cost variances that you can calculate from this, with explanations of any significant ones. I'd be grateful if you could let me have this by close of business tomorrow.

Cost data for week ended 8 July 1998 - double duvet covers in Cutting department

Output
Budgeted double covers produced in the week = 1,900; actual double covers produced in the week = 1,760.

Materials
Cotton used = 11,350 metres, costing £21,565.

Direct labour
Cutting department = 90 hours of Grade 1 labour, costing £402.

Machine hours
Cutting department = 560 machine hours

Overhead
Production overhead charged to Cutting department = £1,650.

SAMPLE SIMULATION

Recording Cost Information

ANSWER BOOKLET

Task 1

STORES LEDGER ACCOUNT

Material description: *Plastic poppers, boxes of 100*

Code no: *PP29*

Maximum quantity:	*180*
Minimum quantity:	*62*
Reorder level:	*95*
Reorder quantity:	*100*

Date	Receipts			Issues			Stock balance		
	Quantity	Price per box £	Total £	Quantity	Price per box £	Total £	Quantity	Price per box £	Total £
1 March							*75*	*62.50*	*4,687.50*

STORES LEDGER ACCOUNT

Material description: *Cotton, 50m rolls*

Code no: *C733*

Maximum quantity:	*175*	
Minimum quantity:	*55*	
Reorder level:	*75*	
Reorder quantity:	*90*	

Date	Receipts			Issues			Stock balance		
	Quantity	Price per box £	Total £	Quantity	Price per box £	Total £	Quantity	Price per box £	Total £
1 March							*65*	*85.50*	*5,557.50*

Task 2

MEMO

To:
From:
Date:
Subject:

MEMO

Task 3

TIMESHEET

Week ending   *6 March 1998*

Employee name   *Amy Harding*   **Employee number**   *2173*

Department   *Finishing*   **Employee grade**   *2*

Activity	Monday Hours	Tuesday Hours	Wednesday Hours	Thursday Hours	Friday Hours	Total Hours
Machining	*7*	*10*	*4*		*4*	
Holiday			*4*	*8*		
Waiting for work	*1*					
Training					*4*	
Total hours payable for day	*8*	*10*	*8*	*8*	*8*	
Number of covers produced	*65*	*72*	*30*	*0*	*32*	

Bonus payable @ £0.15 per cover above 60 per day

Signed   *Amy Harding*   **Manager**   *Jim Stubbs*

Analysis for week	Hours	Rate per hour £	Wages cost £
Direct wages			
Indirect wages			
Basic hours			
Overtime premium			
Bonus			

Task 3, continued

TIMESHEET

Week ending   *6 March 1998*

Employee name   *Jane Amber*   **Employee number**   *2487*

Department   *Cutting*   **Employee grade**   *1*

Activity	Monday Hours	Tuesday Hours	Wednes-day Hours	Thursday Hours	Friday Hours	Total Hours
Cutting	*10*	*6*	*6*		*8*	
Waiting for work		*3*	*2*			
Sick				*8*		
Training					*2*	
Total hours payable for day	*10*	*8*	*8*	*8*	*10*	
Number of covers produced	*70*	*51*	*62*	*0*	*62*	

Bonus payable @ £0.15 per cover above 60 per day

Signed   *Jane Amber*   **Manager**   *Jim Stubbs*

Analysis for week	Hours	Rate per hour £	Wages cost £
Direct wages			
Indirect wages			
Basic hours			
Overtime premium			
Bonus	_____		_____
	_____		_____

Task 3, continued

COST LEDGER DATA ENTRY SHEET

Week ending

Debit accounts

	Cost centre code	Expenditure code	Amount to be debited £
	C100	E300	
	C200	E300	
	C300	E300	
	C400	E300	
	C100	E310	
	C200	E310	
	C300	E310	
	C400	E310	

Check total: total wages for the two employees

Task 4

MEMO

To:
From:
Date:
Subject:

Task 5

MEMO

To:
From:
Date:
Subject:

Task 6

OVERHEAD ANALYSIS SHEET: 1998/99						
Overhead expense: primary apportionments and allocations	Basis of allocation/ apportionment	Total £	Cutting dept £	Finishing dept £	Packing dept £	Stores £

Total of primary allocations

Re-apportion stores

Total production cost centre overhead

Machine hours

Direct labour hours

Overhead absorption rate for 1998/99

Task 7a

MEMO

To:
From:
Date:
Subject:

Task 7b, c, d

Working sheet for calculation of overhead under/over absorbed

Packing department, quarter ending 30 June 1998

7(b) Production overhead absorbed £ _____

7(c) Actual production overhead incurred £ _____

7(d) Production overhead under or over absorbed, to be
transferred to profit and loss account £ _____

Task 8

STANDARD COST CARD 1998/99

Product: Box of 6 double duvet covers
Product code no: 00214

Description	Material code no/direct labour grade	Quantity	Std price £ per metre/ hour etc	Total £
Direct materials				
Cotton fabric	CT33	38.2 metres		
Plastic poppers	PP29	60		
Polyester thread	TP72	22 metres		
Packing - cardboard box	PB03	1 box		
Other materials	Various	-	-	0.81
Subtotal, direct materials			(A)	
Direct labour				
Cutting	Grade 1	0.35 hours		
Finishing	Grade 1	4.10 hours		
Packing	Grade 3	0.50 hours		
Subtotal, direct labour			(B)	
Production overhead				
Cutting department		1.80 machine hours		
Finishing department		4.10 labour hours		
Packing department		0.50 labour hours		
Subtotal, production overhead			(C)	
Total standard production cost			(A + B + C)	

Task 9

MEMO

To:
From:
Date:
Subject:

Workings

Practice devolved assessment
1 *Country Custom Kitchens*

Performance criteria

The following performance criteria are covered in this Devolved Assessment.

Element 5.1: Record and analyse information relating to direct costs

1   Direct costs are identified in accordance with the organisation's costing procedures

2   Information relating to direct costs is clearly and correctly coded, analysed and recorded

3   Direct costs are calculated in accordance with the organisation's policies and procedures

4   Standard costs are compared against actual costs and any variances are analysed

5   Information is systematically checked against the overall usage and stock control practices

6   Queries are either resolved or referred to the appropriate person

Notes on completing the Assessment

This Assessment is designed to test your ability to record and analyse information relating to direct costs.

You are provided with data on Pages 190 to 203 which you must use to complete the tasks on Page 190.

You are allowed **three hours** to complete your work.

A high level of accuracy is required. Check your work carefully.

Correcting fluid should not be used. Errors should be crossed out neatly and clearly. You should write in ink - not pencil.

A full suggested solution to this Assessment is provided on Page 295.

Do not turn to the suggested solution until you have completed all parts of the Assessment.

PRACTICE DEVOLVED ASSESSMENT 1: COUNTRY CUSTOM KITCHENS

Data

Following a chip-pan fire in its warehouse showroom, the computerised stock control system of Country Custom Kitchens is out of action. The management of Country Custom Kitchens has called in your firm to help restore the system and you and a number of your colleagues have been delegated the task of keeping the system running manually while the computer system and records are being rebuilt. This is likely to take up to two weeks.

When you arrive on Monday 6 September you find that you are to look after raw materials stocks in the code range A - F (screws and fixings). You are given the A - F part of the daily stock list which was run on the evening before the fire. No transactions have been posted since then. The stock list gives the usual details and also has an 'exceptions' column signalling stocks that need to be reordered. The cost accountant has left you a note about this (she suffered minor burns and is recuperating).

You are handed a pile of documents received or generated that morning. You sort the documents into separate piles and find that you have the following:

(a) The stock list

(b) Several invoices

(c) A number of goods received notes (all of which match their attached purchase orders) for that morning's deliveries

(d) Some materials requisition notes

(e) The note from the cost accountant

Tasks

Using the documents and information on the following pages, complete the tasks outlined below.

(a) Make out stores ledger accounts as necessary and write them up in the light of the documents that you have been given. There is no need to enter control levels on the stores ledger accounts, but otherwise see that all documents (including the materials requisitions) are as complete as possible. If you have any queries note them down on a queries schedule.

(b) (i) Peruse the stock list and make out purchase requisitions for any items that need to be reordered.

(ii) Suggest a way of ensuring that stocks that you requisition are not ordered again once the computer system is restored.

Again, if you are unsure of anything make a note of it.

(c) Peruse the stock list generally and note down on your queries schedule any points that you think need to be brought to the attention of the warehouse manager or the chief purchasing officer.

(d) Prepare journal entries for posting the invoices to the integrated accounts. (Do not prepare entries for variances.)

(e) Calculate any variances that have arisen.

(f) Note on your queries schedule any other matters that you think need to be referred to other persons.

(g) Prepare a schedule of materials issued for job costing purposes.

Documents for use in the solution

The documents you will need to prepare a solution are given on Pages 204 to 214 and consist of the following.

(a) Materials requisitions (to be completed)
(b) 12 blank stores ledger accounts
(c) 7 blank purchase requisitions
(d) 1 blank looseleaf journal page

COUNTRY CUSTOM KITCHENS STOCK LIST 03/09/X3 — 03/09/X3/ 17:52

CODE	DESCRIPTION		FACTOR/UNIT	SUPPLIER	COST	IN	OUT	ORDERED	BALANCE	EXCE-PTION	TRANS......ACTIONS PREV.TOTAL	HISTORY PREV.CUM.	CURRENT CUM.
A0080	SCREW AND NUT	50mm	5	28043112	0.49				58		562	421	383
A0090	SCREW AND NUT	60mm	5	28043112	0.53				63		668	455	445
A1010	WING NUT	M4	5	27561297	0.40				38		452	263	289
A1020	WING NUT	M5	5	27561297	0.40				68		666	454	363
A1030	WING NUT	M6	5	27561297	0.45				54		523	370	362
A1040	WING NUT	M8	5	27561297	0.50		20		34		360	236	259
A1050	SUPANUT	M4	10	23344248	0.27			10	7		166	124	148
A1060	SUPANUT	M5	10	23344248	0.30				48		571	389	353
A1070	SUPANUT	M6	10	23344248	0.32				95		1007	587	469
A1080	SUPANUT	M8	10	23344248	0.37	80			88		862	587	645
A1090	SUPANUT	M10	5	23344248	0.40	70			86		834	549	439
A2010	WASHER	15mm	50	28043112	0.25	70			82		976	732	717
A2020	WASHER	20mm	50	28043112	0.30	70			32		339	197	157
A2030	WASHER	25mm	50	28043112	0.33				70		679	480	528
A2040	WASHER	30mm	20	28043112	0.37	80			99		1049	715	650
A2050	WASHER	35mm	10	28043112	0.30				59		578	380	456
A2060	WASHER BRASS	15mm	10	28043112	0.40		60		1	***	740	493	487
A2070	WASHER BRASS	20mm	5	27561247	0.45		30		13	***	605	393	399
A2080	WASHER BRASS	25mm	5	27561247	0.50				62		607	429	343
A2090	WASHER BRASS	30mm	5	27561247	0.55	80			86		1023	596	655
A3010	SELF-TAP	15mm	10	23344248	0.21				16		170	127	115
A3020	SELF-TAP	20mm	10	23344248	0.24			15	17		148	100	98
A3030	SELF-TAP	25mm	10	23344248	0.27				52		509	335	368
A3040	SELF-TAP	30mm	10	23344248	0.30				74		647	441	529
A3050	SELF-TAP	35mm	10	23344248	0.33			80	18		1166	680	618
A3060	SELF-TAP	40mm	5	23344248	0.30				40		350	247	242
A3070	SELF-TAP	45mm	5	23344248	0.33				72		698	523	271
A3080	SELF-TAP	50mm	5	23344248	0.36				61		647	425	510
A3090	SELF-TAP	60mm	5	23344248	0.39				21		183	124	136
A4010	ROUNDHEAD	15mm	10	28043112	0.22				61		591	344	337
A4020	ROUNDHEAD	20mm	10	28043112	0.24				57		678	480	528
A4030	ROUNDHEAD	25mm	10	28043112	0.26				74		725	477	434
A4040	ROUNDHEAD	30mm	10	28043112	0.28		50		13	***	760	500	475

COUNTRY CUSTOM KITCHENS STOCK LIST 03/09/X3 — 03/09/X3 / 17:52

CODE	DESCRIPTION	FACTOR/UNIT	SUPPLIER	COST	IN	OUT	ORDERED	BALANCE	EXCE-PTION	TRANS...ACTIONS PREV.TOTAL	HISTORY PREV.CUM.	CURRENT.CUM.
A4050	ROUNDHEAD	35mm	10	28043112	0.30				78		827	544	533
A4060	ROUNDHEAD	40mm	5	23344248	0.20			30	10		372	279	223
A4070	ROUNDHEAD	45mm	5	23344248	0.24			75	50		892	520	572
A4080	ROUNDHEAD	50mm	5	23344248	0.28		50		12	***	800	520	533
A4090	ROUNDHEAD	60mm	5	23344248	0.32				15		481	316	309
A5010	CROSSHEAD	15mm	10	27561297	0.18			40	66		785	535	588
A5020	CROSSHEAD	20mm	10	27561297	0.19				80		784	555	505
A5030	CROSSHEAD	25mm	10	27561297	0.20				131		1389	914	895
A5040	CROSSHEAD	30mm	10	27561297	0.21	100			84		823	617	678
A5050	CROSSHEAD	35mm	10	27561297	0.23				76		737	429	343
A5060	CROSSHEAD	40mm	5	28043112	0.17				25		298	211	232
A5070	CROSSHEAD	45mm	5	28043112	0.20				21		205	134	107
A5080	CROSSHEAD	50mm	5	28043112	0.24				96		840	572	632
A5090	CROSSHEAD	60mm	5	28043112	0.30				93		985	544	1182
A6010	BRASS	15mm	10	29295001	0.35				96		940	705	641
A6020	BRASS	20mm	10	29295001	0.39				32		310	204	199
A6030	BRASS	25mm	10	29295001	0.41				36		428	303	333
A6040	BRASS	30mm	10	29295001	0.43				96		941	548	438
A6050	BRASS	35mm	10	29295001	0.46				57		552	376	342
A6060	BRASS	40mm	5	29295001	0.46			40	21		492	340	341
A6070	BRASS	45mm	10	29295001	0.56			50	29		610	400	417
A6080	BRASS	50mm	5	29295001	0.62				77		916	603	482
A6090	BRASS	60mm	5	29295001	0.74				72		705	480	436
*****												
B0010	RLH NAILS	20mm	1kg	23344248	2.69				74		148	148	0
B0020	RLH NAILS	25mm	1kg	23344248	2.69				51		153	153	0
B0030	RLH NAILS	30mm	1kg	23344248	2.69		4	10	0		107	72	79
B0040	RLH NAILS	35mm	1kg	23344248	2.79				24		235	154	150
B0050	RLH NAILS	40mm	1kg	23344248	2.79		6		16		155	109	186
B0060	RLH NAILS	45mm	1kg	23344248	2.99				56		666	388	353
B0070	RLH NAILS	50mm	1kg	23344248	2.99				27		264	173	138
B0080	N/A												
B0090	N/A												

COUNTRY CUSTOM KITCHENS STOCK LIST 03/09/X3 — 03/09/X3 / 17:52

CODE	DESCRIPTION	FACTOR/UNIT	SUPPLIER	COST	IN	OUT	ORDERED	BALANCE	EXCE-PTION	TRANS......ACTIONS PREV.TOTAL	PREV.CUM.	HISTORY CURRENT.CUM.
B1010	RW NAILS	15mm	1kg	27314295	2.60				40		424	280	130
B1020	RW NAILS	20mm	1kg	27314295	2.60				49		568	520	212
B1030	RW NAILS	25mm	1kg	27314295	2.60				19		186	139	136
B1040	RW NAILS	30mm	1kg	27314295	2.60				29		281	184	167
B1050	RW NAILS	35mm	1kg	27314295	2.90				22		262	152	314
B1060	RW NAILS	40mm	1kg	27314295	2.90		5		12		105	74	81
B1070	RW NAILS	45mm	1kg	27314295	2.99		5	60	11		695	457	447
B1080	RW NAILS	50mm	1kg	27314295	3.05				61		85	83	14
B1090	RW NAILS	60mm	1kg	27314295	3.15				93		200	179	7
B2010	PANEL PINS	15mm	500g	27561297	1.89				34		405	266	292
B2020	PANEL PINS	20mm	500g	27561297	1.89				14		135	101	111
B2030	PANEL PINS	25mm	500g	27561297	1.99		35		42		403	250	268
B2040	PANEL PINS	30mm	500g	27561297	1.99				49		428	249	273
B2050	PANEL PINS	35mm	500g	27314295	1.99		4		30		357	243	238
B2060	PANEL PINS	40mm	500g	27314295	2.15				11		106	69	75
B2070	PANEL PINS	45mm	500g	27314295	2.15			20	2		222	157	125
B2080	PANEL PINS	50mm	500g	27314295	2.40				7		61	45	54
B2090	PANEL PINS	60mm	500g	27314295	2.40				31		369	242	266
*****												
D0010	BUTT HINGE	40mm	5PR	26134906	1.89	15			89		180	118	54
D0020	BUTT HINGE	50mm	5PR	26134906	2.70				0	***	16	16	1
D0030	BUTT HINGE	65mm	5PR	26134096	3.45				2	***	19	18	0
D0040	BUTT HINGE	75mm	5PR	26134096	5.27				26		252	171	155
D0050	BUTT HINGE	100mm	5PR	26134096	9.99				26		254	167	163
D0060	BUTT CHR	40mm	5PR	23344248	3.14				11		131	92	104
D0070	BUTT CHR	50mm	5PR	23344248	3.73				22		192	146	143
D0080	BUTT CHR	75mm	5PR	23344248	6.84				38		403	265	241
D0090	BUTT CHR	100mm	5PR	23344248	11.87		10	10	8		174	118	141
D1010	RISING BUTT	40mm	5PR	26134906	1.70				8		78	45	49
D1020	RISING BUTT	50mm	5PR	26134906	2.20				3	***	38	29	0
D1030	RISING BUTT	65mm	5PR	26134906	2.56				2	***	47	43	2
D1040	RISING BUTT	75mm	5PR	26134906	4.32				19		166	109	119
D1050	RISING BUTT	100mm	5PR	26134906	8.87				9		107	75	73

COUNTRY CUSTOM KITCHENS STOCK LIST 03/09/X3   03/09/X3/ 17:52

CODE	DESCRIPTION		FACTOR/UNIT	SUPPLIER	COST	IN	OUT	ORDERED	BALANCE	EXCEPTION	TRANS.....ACTIONS PREV.TOTAL	HISTORY PREV. CUM.	CURRENT CUM.
D1060	RIS.BUTT.CHR	40mm	5PR	23344248	2.99				14		148	111	133
D1070	RIS.BUTT.CHR	50mm	5PR	23344248	3.49				17		164	107	97
D1080	RIS.BUTT.CHR	75mm	5PR	23344248	7.50				17		166	113	110
D1090	RIS.BUTT.CHR	100mm	5PR	23344248	12.00				15		131	76	83
D2010	LIFT OFF BUTT	40mm	5PR	21840027	3.07	10			30		357	267	213
D2020	LIFT OFF BUTT	50mm	5PR	21840027	3.99				38		368	242	237
D2030	LIFT OFF BUTT	65mm	5PR	21840027	4.58		20		2	***	204	130	140
D2040	LIFT OFF BUTT	75mm	5PR	21840027	6.90				19		201	137	124
D2050	LIFT OFF BUTT	100mm	5PR	21840027	12.00				13		127	74	72
D2060	L/O BUTT CHROME	40mm	5PR	23344248	4.05			10	8		214	151	166
D2070	L/O BUTT CHROME	50mm	5PR	23344248	6.07			10	4		122	80	96
D2080	L/O BUTT CHROME	75mm	5PR	23344248	8.17			10	4		137	102	81
D2090	L/O BUTT CHROME	100mm	5PR	23344248	14.92		3		6		64	37	40
D3010	CRANKED LIFT OFF	38mm	1PR	27561297	1.35				8		77	54	52
D3020	EASY HANG	50mm	1PR	29295001	1.45				22		262	172	156
D3030	EASY FIX ANTIQUE	50mm	1PR	27314295	0.99		20	35	0		417	274	328
D3040	CONCEALED	26mm	1PR	28043112	2.59	50			64		627	427	341
D3050	CONCEALED	35mm	1PR	28043112	3.35	75			85		901	593	652
D3060	CONCEALED	170°	1PR	28043112	8.95	50			75		656	464	371
D3070	PIANO	350mm	1	25567840	2.12				33		323	188	184
D3080	PIANO	700mm	1	25567840	3.99	75			26		309	203	184
D3090	PIANO	900mm	1	25567840	4.35		1		13		126	85	102
*****													
F0010	CAVITY FIXINGS	C23	12	27314295	2.89	60			78		827	563	450
F0020	CAVITY FIXINGS	C29	12	26134906	1.24				30		294	193	212
F0030	CAVITY FIXINGS	H54	12	29295001	1.99				51		607	354	346
F0040	CAVITY FIXINGS	F42	12	25567840	1.59	50		50	73		638	451	410
F0050	PLASTIC PLUGS	25mm	100	27561297	1.19				76		737	485	582
F0060	PLASTIC PLUGS	35mm	100	27561297	1.49	75			90		954	715	786
F0070	PLASTIC PLUGS	40mm	100	27561297	1.99				71		695	405	396
F0080	PLASTIC PLUGS	45mm	100	27561297	2.05				32		361	246	196
F0090	PLASTIC PLUGS	50mm	100	27561297	2.47				50		437	287	287
F1010	END BRACKETS	19mm	1PR	27314295	2.29		4		10		97	68	74

COUNTRY CUSTOM KITCHENS STOCK LIST 03/09/X3 — 03/09/X3 / 17:52

CODE	DESCRIPTION		FACTOR/UNIT	SUPPLIER	COST	IN	OUT	ORDERED	BALANCE	EXCE-PTION	TRANS......ACTIONS PREV.TOTAL	HISTORY PREV.CUM.	CURRENT CUM.
F1020	END BRACKETS	25mm	1PR	27314295	2.47				0	***	148	97	17
F1030	END BRACKETS	25mm	1PR	27314295	2.47			10	4		6	3	90
F1040	CENTRE BRACKET	19mm	1	27314295	1.79		1		2		20	11	10
F1050	CENTRE BRACKET	25mm	1	27314295	2.20		2		2		23	17	20
F1060	STEEL TUBE	19mm	2m	28043112	5.59		1		2		19	12	10
F1070	STEEL TUBE	25mm	2m	28043112	7.07				1	***	14	9	9
F1080	BRASS TUBE	19mm	2m	28043112	8.23				5		43	24	26
F1090	BRASS TUBE	25mm	2m	28043112	10.00				8		85	60	58
F2010	DRAWER RUNNERS		1PR	29295001	2.49				122		1452	955	764
F2020	CORNER FITTINGS		4	29295001	3.29				79		774	527	579
F2030	EXTERNAL ANGLE		2m	23344248	1.65				50		485	282	256
F2040	EXTERNAL ANGLE	19mm	2m	23344248	1.99	300		200	113		2028	1436	1723
F2050	CLIP ON EDGING	25mm	2m	26134906	2.49				350		3710	2782	3060
F2060	FLAT EDGING		2m	26134906	1.35				167		1987	1308	1046
F2070	LIPPED EDGING		2m	26134906	1.55				105		1029	728	662
F2080	DOOR TRACK		2m	26134906	11.79		20		140		1225	714	785
F2090	SINGLE CHANNEL	17mm	2m	26134906	2.29				185		1961	1336	1309
F3010	SINGLE CHANNEL	6mm	2m	26134906	1.15				216		2116	1587	1904
F3020	S/A TRIM	W	2m	27314295	1.50		25		175		2083	1371	1247
F3030	S/A TRIM		2m	27314295	1.50				220		2620	1747	1654
F3040	S/A TRIM	B	2m	27314295	1.50			125	27		1611	939	1032
F3050	DEC. MOULDINGS		4	25567840	1.65				67		649	459	550
F3060	DEC. CORNERS		4	25567840	2.29				35		417	274	268
F3070	DEC. CROWNS		4	25567840	4.79			10	7		148	111	101
F3080	DEC. BRACKET		4	25567840	3.75				0	***	5	5	1
F3090	DEC. TRIM		2m	25567840	3.99				0	***	12	12	2
F4010	BICYCLE HOOKS		1PR	28043112	0.99				55		533	310	341
F1020	UNIV. HOOKS		1PR	28043112	1.49				46		450	306	244
F4030	CUP HOOKS		4	28043112	0.45				89		778	512	614
F4040	CUP HOOKS BRASSED		4	28043112	0.28				70		679	480	528
F4050	HOOK AND EYES		1	28043112	0.41	800	400		923		10984	7231	5073
F4060	SCREW HOOK		1	28043112	0.77		50		360		4284	3213	2923
F4070	VINE EYES		10	28043112	1.89				40		350	204	199

COUNTRY CUSTOM KITCHENS STOCK LIST 03/09/X3   03/09/X3 / 17:52

CODE	DESCRIPTION	FACTOR/UNIT	SUPPLIER	COST	IN	OUT	ORDERED	BALANCE	EXCE-PTION	TRANS......ACTIONS PREV.TOTAL	HISTORY PREV.CUM.	CURRENT.CUM.
F4080	SCREWEYES	19mm	25	27314295	0.76			60	12		763	520	624
F4090	SCREWEYES	25mm	25	27314295	0.89				12		116	82	90
F5010	MAGN.CATCH	W	1	27561297	3.99				45		441	300	240
F5020	MAGN.CATCH	B	1	27561297	3.99				44		385	253	229
F5030	MAGN.CATCH	S	1	27561297	3.99				43		512	384	376
F5040	SLIDE LATCH	W	1	23344248	4.79				40		388	226	271
F5050	SLIDE LATCH	B	1	23344248	4.79			40	7		460	325	357
F5060	THUMBLATCH	W	1	23344248	3.99				36		315	214	194
F5070	THUMBLATCH	B	1	23344248	3.99				37		358	208	166
F5080	AUTOLATCH	W	1	23344248	2.69				36		428	281	275
F5090	AUTOLATCH	B	1	23344248	2.69				68		595	446	490
F6010	PEG CASTORS	$\frac{3}{4}$"	4	26134906	2.39				32		310	219	250
F6020	PEG CASTORS	1"	4	26134906	2.56				8		85	57	51
F6030	PEG CASTORS	$1\frac{1}{4}$"	4	26134906	2.78				7		61	40	32
F6040	PLATE CASTORS	$\frac{3}{4}$"	4	26134906	2.39				9		78	53	51
F6050	PLATE CASTORS	1"	4	26134906	2.56				5		58	33	36
F6060	PLATE CASTORS	$1\frac{1}{4}$"	4	26134906	2.78				5		48	36	43
F6070	BUGGY WHEEL	$1\frac{1}{2}$"	4	25567840	1.45			4	9		78	51	46
F6080	BUGGY WHEEL	2"	4	25567840	1.99			4	5		53	37	29
F6090	DEC.CASTORS		4	25567840	3.50				6		58	39	42
F7010	TOOL CLIP	20mm	1	29295001	0.35				10		118	77	92
F7020	TOOL CLIP	38mm	1	29295001	0.50				35		306	208	189
F7030	HOSE CLIP	20mm	1	29295001	0.46				78		764	445	489
F7040	HOSE CLIP	38mm	1	29295001	0.46	60			89		943	667	653
F7050	HOSE CLIP	50mm	1	29295001	0.53				20		194	127	101
F7060	G.CLIP	15mm	1	28043112	0.18				41		401	300	273
F7070	G.CLIP	20mm	1	28043112	0.20				60		525	306	336
F7080	G.CLIP	25mm	1	28043112	0.23				68		809	573	687
F7090	G.CLIP	30mm	1	28043112	0.25				48		465	306	278
F8010	DOORSTOP-CONC		1	21840027	0.66				25		245	167	133
F8020	DOORSTOP-FLEX		2	21840027	1.29				19		166	117	128
F8030	DOORSTOP-RUB		1	21840027	0.75				37		392	258	252

CHIPPIES
Veneers
Splinter's Yard, Glue Street
Deighton

Country Custom
 Kitchens
Brightwell Road
Croydon

INVOICE

Order N./Ref 2073   Inv. No. 76298   Date 03.09.X3

Quantity	Description	Unit Price		Total	
		£	p	£	p
1000	Ash veneer 500cm panels	4	70	4,700	00
		Sub-total		4,700	00
		VAT @ 17.5%		822	50
		Invoice total		5,522	50

VAT Reg: 88458485

PERKALLS FIXINGS

Pink Street, Dartford, Kent

Country Custom
 Kitchens
Brightwell Road
Croydon

INVOICE

Order No./Ref 2072   Inv. No. 1187   Date 03.09.X3

Quantity	Description	Unit Price £	p	Total £	p
50	F42 R/P	1	68	84	00
4	Buggy wheel	2	07	8	28
	Sub-total			92	28
	VAT @ 17.5%			16	15
	Invoice total			108	43

VAT Reg No: 17128987

KEWANBY SUPPLIES
THE EDGE OFTOWN, WARE

Country Custom
Kitchens
Brightwell Road
Croydon

INVOICE

O/N - 2178   Inv. No. 87/61743   Date 03.09.X3

Quantity	Description	Unit Price £	p	Total £	p
15	Self-tap 20mm	0	24	3	60
75	Roundhead 45mm	0	24	18	00
40	Roundhead 60mm	0	35	14	00
80	Self-tap 35mm	0	35	28	00
10	Round lost heads 30mm	2	72	27	20
40	Slide latch (black)	4	95	198	00
10	Chromium lift off 50mm	6	20	62	00
	Sub-total			350	80
	VAT @ 17.5%			61	39
	Invoice total			412	19

VAT Reg No: 09347219

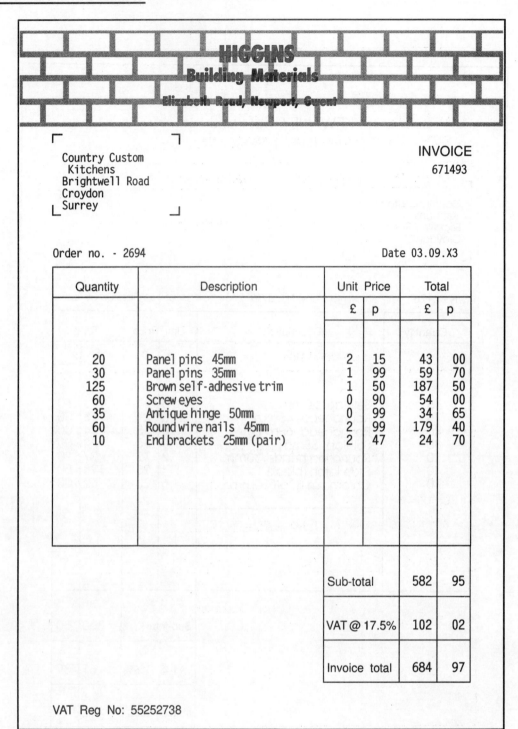

HIGGINS
Building Materials
Elizabeth Road, Newport, Gwent

Country Custom
 Kitchens
Brightwell Road
Croydon
 Surrey

INVOICE
671493

Order no. - 2694   Date 03.09.X3

Quantity	Description	Unit Price		Total	
		£	p	£	p
20	Panel pins 45mm	2	15	43	00
30	Panel pins 35mm	1	99	59	70
125	Brown self-adhesive trim	1	50	187	50
60	Screw eyes	0	90	54	00
35	Antique hinge 50mm	0	99	34	65
60	Round wire nails 45mm	2	99	179	40
10	End brackets 25mm (pair)	2	47	24	70
	Sub-total			582	95
	VAT @ 17.5%			102	02
	Invoice total			684	97

VAT Reg No: 55252738

GOODS RECEIVED NOTE WAREHOUSE COPY

DATE: 6.9.X3   TIME: 9.15   NO 24638

ORDER NO: 2164

SUPPLIER'S ADVICE NOTE NO: AN067

QUANTITY	CAT NO	DESCRIPTION
10		Chrome hinges 75mm
		Stock code D2080

RECEIVED IN GOOD CONDITION: JB   (INITIALS)

GOODS RECEIVED NOTE WAREHOUSE COPY

DATE: 6.9.X3   TIME: 9.25   NO 24639

ORDER NO: 2170

SUPPLIER'S ADVICE NOTE NO: PRB/73

QUANTITY	CAT NO	DESCRIPTION
50 (5 packs)		Brass screws 45mm
		Stock code A6070

RECEIVED IN GOOD CONDITION: JB   (INITIALS)

GOODS RECEIVED NOTE WAREHOUSE COPY

DATE: 6.9.X3   TIME: 10.10   NO 24670

ORDER NO: 2154

SUPPLIER'S ADVICE NOTE NO: 10423

QUANTITY	CAT NO	DESCRIPTION
10 (4 pkt)		Decorative crowns

Stock code ?

RECEIVED IN GOOD CONDITION: JB   (INITIALS)

GOODS RECEIVED NOTE WAREHOUSE COPY

DATE: 6.9.X3   TIME: 11.05   NO 24671

ORDER NO: 2184

SUPPLIER'S ADVICE NOTE NO: NONE

QUANTITY	CAT NO	DESCRIPTION
10 (10 pkt)		Super Nut M4

Stock code A1050

RECEIVED IN GOOD CONDITION: JB   (INITIALS)

GOODS RECEIVED NOTE WAREHOUSE COPY

DATE: 6.9.X3   TIME: 11.05   NO 24672

ORDER NO: 2184

SUPPLIER'S ADVICE NOTE NO: NONE

QUANTITY	CAT NO	DESCRIPTION
200 (2m lengths)		Angle 19mm

Stock code | F2040

RECEIVED IN GOOD CONDITION: JB   (INITIALS)

GOODS RECEIVED NOTE WAREHOUSE COPY

DATE: 6.9.X3   TIME: 11.05   NO 24673

ORDER NO: 2184

SUPPLIER'S ADVICE NOTE NO: NONE

QUANTITY	CAT NO	DESCRIPTION
30 (5 pkt)		Roundhead screws 40mm

Stock code |

RECEIVED IN GOOD CONDITION: JB   (INITIALS)

MATERIALS REQUISITION

Material Required for: *K309/93*
(Job or Overhead Account)

No. 0914

Date: *6.9.X3*

Quantity	Description	Code No.	Factor/ Unit	Rate	£	Notes
15	Steel washer 30mm					

Foreman: *Vlad Kopeii*   Costed and Coded:

MATERIALS REQUISITION

Material Required for: *K309/93*
(Job or Overhead Account)

No. 0915

Date: *6.9.X3*

Quantity	Description	Code No.	Factor/ Unit	Rate	£	Notes
10	R/Hd 30mm					

Foreman: *Vlad Kopeii*   Costed and Coded:

MATERIALS REQUISITION

Material Required for: *K312/93*
(Job or Overhead Account)

No. 0916

Date: *6.9.X3*

Quantity	Description	Code No.	Factor/ Unit	Rate	£	Notes
10 chrome	Butt hinges 40mm					

Foreman: *VK*   Costed and Coded:

MATERIALS REQUISITION

Material Required for: *K313/93*   No. 0917
(Job or Overhead Account)

Date: *6.9.X3*

Quantity	Description	Code No.	Factor/ Unit	Rate	£	Notes
8	Drawer runners					

Foreman: *VK*   Costed and Coded:

MATERIALS REQUISITION

Material Required for: *K313/93*   No. 0918
(Job or Overhead Account)

Date: *6.9.X3*

Quantity	Description	Code No.	Factor/ Unit	Rate	£	Notes
20	White magnetic catches					

Foreman: *Vlad*   Costed and Coded:

MATERIALS REQUISITION

Material Required for: *K309/93*   No. 0919
(Job or Overhead Account)

Date: *6.9.X3*

Quantity	Description	Code No.	Factor/ Unit	Rate	£	Notes
2	Panel pins 35mm					

Foreman: *VK*   Costed and Coded:

STORES LEDGER ACCOUNT

Material: _____ Maximum Quantity: _____

Code: _____ Minimum Quantity: _____

Date	Receipts				Issues				Stock		
	G.R.N. No.	Quantity	Unit Price £	Amount £	Stores Req. No.	Quantity	Unit Price £	Amount £	Quantity	Unit Price £	Amount £

STORES LEDGER ACCOUNT

Material: _____ Maximum Quantity: _____

Code: _____ Minimum Quantity: _____

Date	Receipts				Issues				Stock		
	G.R.N. No.	Quantity	Unit Price £	Amount £	Stores Req. No.	Quantity	Unit Price £	Amount £	Quantity	Unit Price £	Amount £

STORES LEDGER ACCOUNT

Material: _____ Maximum Quantity: _____

Code: _____ Minimum Quantity: _____

Date	Receipts				Issues				Stock		
	G.R.N. No.	Quantity	Unit Price £	Amount £	Stores Req. No.	Quantity	Unit Price £	Amount £	Quantity	Unit Price £	Amount £

STORES LEDGER ACCOUNT

Material: .... Maximum Quantity: ....

Code: .... Minimum Quantity: ....

Date	Receipts				Issues				Stock		
	G.R.N. No.	Quantity	Unit Price £	Amount £	Stores Req. No.	Quantity	Unit Price £	Amount £	Quantity	Unit Price £	Amount £

STORES LEDGER ACCOUNT

Material: .... Maximum Quantity: ....

Code: .... Minimum Quantity: ....

Date	Receipts				Issues				Stock		
	G.R.N. No.	Quantity	Unit Price £	Amount £	Stores Req. No.	Quantity	Unit Price £	Amount £	Quantity	Unit Price £	Amount £

STORES LEDGER ACCOUNT

Material: .... Maximum Quantity: ....

Code: .... Minimum Quantity: ....

Date	Receipts				Issues				Stock		
	G.R.N. No.	Quantity	Unit Price £	Amount £	Stores Req. No.	Quantity	Unit Price £	Amount £	Quantity	Unit Price £	Amount £

STORES LEDGER ACCOUNT

Material: .... Maximum Quantity: ....

Code: .... Minimum Quantity: ....

Date	Receipts				Issues				Stock		
	G.R.N. No.	Quantity	Unit Price £	Amount £	Stores Req. No.	Quantity	Unit Price £	Amount £	Quantity	Unit Price £	Amount £

STORES LEDGER ACCOUNT

Material: .... Maximum Quantity: ....

Code: .... Minimum Quantity: ....

Date	Receipts				Issues				Stock		
	G.R.N. No.	Quantity	Unit Price £	Amount £	Stores Req. No.	Quantity	Unit Price £	Amount £	Quantity	Unit Price £	Amount £

STORES LEDGER ACCOUNT

Material: .... Maximum Quantity: ....

Code: .... Minimum Quantity: ....

Date	Receipts				Issues				Stock		
	G.R.N. No.	Quantity	Unit Price £	Amount £	Stores Req. No.	Quantity	Unit Price £	Amount £	Quantity	Unit Price £	Amount £

STORES LEDGER ACCOUNT

Material: .... Maximum Quantity: ....

Code: .... Minimum Quantity: ....

Date	Receipts				Issues				Stock		
	G.R.N. No.	Quantity	Unit Price £	Amount £	Stores Req. No.	Quantity	Unit Price £	Amount £	Quantity	Unit Price £	Amount £

STORES LEDGER ACCOUNT

Material: .... Maximum Quantity: ....

Code: .... Minimum Quantity: ....

Date	Receipts				Issues				Stock		
	G.R.N. No.	Quantity	Unit Price £	Amount £	Stores Req. No.	Quantity	Unit Price £	Amount £	Quantity	Unit Price £	Amount £

STORES LEDGER ACCOUNT

Material: .... Maximum Quantity: ....

Code: .... Minimum Quantity: ....

Date	Receipts				Issues				Stock		
	G.R.N. No.	Quantity	Unit Price £	Amount £	Stores Req. No.	Quantity	Unit Price £	Amount £	Quantity	Unit Price £	Amount £

PURCHASE REQUISITION   Req. No.   10427

Department _____   Date
Suggested Supplier:

                                         Requested by:

Quantity	Code	Description	Estimated Cost	
			Unit	£

Authorised signature:

PURCHASE REQUISITION   Req. No.   10428

Department _____   Date
Suggested Supplier:

                                         Requested by:

Quantity	Code	Description	Estimated Cost	
			Unit	£

Authorised signature:

PURCHASE REQUISITION   Req. No.   10429

Department _____
Suggested Supplier:

Date

Requested by:

Quantity	Code	Description	Estimated Cost	
			Unit	£

Authorised signature:

PURCHASE REQUISITION   Req. No.   10430

Department _____
Suggested Supplier:

Date

Requested by:

Quantity	Code	Description	Estimated Cost	
			Unit	£

Authorised signature:

PURCHASE REQUISITION   Req. No.   10431

Department _____

Suggested Supplier:

Date

Requested by:

Quantity	Code	Description	Estimated Cost	
			Unit	£

Authorised signature:

PURCHASE REQUISITION   Req. No.   10432

Department _____

Suggested Supplier:

Date

Requested by:

Quantity	Code	Description	Estimated Cost	
			Unit	£

Authorised signature:

PURCHASE REQUISITION Req. No.   10433

Department _____   Date
Suggested Supplier:

                                          Requested by:

Quantity	Code	Description	Estimated Cost	
			Unit	£

Authorised signature:

Notes from cost accountant on stock list

'Cost' is Standard cost per packet of 10 (or whatever) as shown in the factor column.

In/Out/Balance etc is number of packets (etc) not number of individual items.

Exceptions: - Stock needing re-ordering

- re-order signalled when less than 1 month's stock on the basis of last year's usage

- re-order qty roughly 1 month's stock (to the nearest five)

- computer over-ridden for slow-moving stock

Prev. total = number of items issued last year

Slow moving stock   - we classify stock as slow moving if the current cumulative number of items issued is significantly lower than the previous year's cumulative

NB Friday's deliveries are all posted but system does not up-date 'ordered' column until next morning (helps with matching invoices)

Otherwise self explanatory

Date	Customer/ supplier code	Invoice	Order No.	Stock code	Quantity	Net £	VAT (17.5%) £

Journal No.

Practice devolved assessment
2 *Stancourt Motors*

Performance criteria

The following performance criteria are covered in this Devolved Assessment.

Element 5.1: Record and analyse information relating to direct costs

1   Direct costs are identified in accordance with the organisation's costing procedures

2   Information relating to direct costs is clearly and correctly coded, analysed and recorded

3   Direct costs are calculated in accordance with the organisation's policies and procedures

6   Queries are either resolved or referred to the appropriate person

Notes on completing the Assessment

This Assessment is designed to test your ability to operate and maintain a system of accounting for labour costs.

You are provided with data on Pages 216 to 228 which you must use to complete the task on Page 216.

You are allowed **two hours** to complete your work.

A high level of accuracy is required. Check your work carefully.

Correcting fluid should not be used. Errors should be crossed out neatly and clearly. You should write in ink - not pencil.

A full suggested solution to this Assessment is provided on Page 311.

Do not turn to the suggested solution until you have completed all parts of the Assessment.

PRACTICE DEVOLVED ASSESSMENT 2: STANCOURT MOTORS

Data

Stancourt Motors is a small car dealer in Birmingham selling new and used cars and repairing and servicing cars of all makes. Your name is Doris and you started work as an accounts assistant in the accounts department just over a week ago.

Late on Tuesday afternoon you learn that you are to be sent over to the repairs and services department because Rex Davison, the costing clerk, has been called away suddenly. There are four job cost cards to be prepared prior to producing invoices for customers due to collect their cars on Wednesday morning.

By the time you arrive in Rex Davison's office he has gone, but there is a sheaf of papers underneath a paperweight and a scribbled note saying 'Doris this is all you need'.

You find the following documents.

(a) A computer produced summary of the original estimates prepared for all customers collecting tomorrow

(b) Four job cards stamped with times, in the style of a clock card

(c) Numerous tear off slips which, on closer examination, turn out to be materials issue slips generated by the computer. These appear to have originally been stapled to the job cards, but in such a way that they have had to be removed so that the details can be read. They have been helpfully rearranged in issue note number order.

(d) A handwritten invoice

Otherwise all you have is your wits and the small amount of knowledge you have gained in your short time working for Stancourt Motors. You know, for example, that the mechanics and body repairers work a 40 hour week, that they are paid weekly and that, if they complete a job in less than the estimated time, they get a bonus equal to the time saved at their standard rate of pay. These bonuses are included in the job costs. You know that there are two cost centres, A for mechanical repairs and B for bodywork.

There is a file of completed job cost cards on Rex's desk. These are very difficult to read, but you manage to establish that indirect expenses seemed to be charged at a rate of £3.50 for every labour hour worked in cost centre A and £2.50 for every labour hour worked in cost centre B. After some study, you deduce that quotations are given on the basis of labour at £18 per hour plus parts at cost. This is the invoiced price unless cost plus 10% is greater.

You also obtain a copy of last week's payroll for the repairs and services department.

Task

Complete the four job cost cards required using the documents on the following pages.

The four blank job cost cards you will need to prepare a solution are given on Pages 218 to 221.

ESTIMATE SUMMARY - CARS GOING OUT 14.6.X3

Estimate No.	Detail	Hours
2574	Remove nearside rear vent. Fit new vent. Flat down near side rear vent. Prime and prepare, respray in colour. Fit new parts as listed below. Refit all removed parts.	4
2583	Investigate knocking thought to be faulty distributor shaft. Re-align centre bearing. Carry out repairs as necessary, but advise customer when fault is known.	2
2589	Repairs to distributor and commutator end frame pursuant to 2583.	3
2594	Remove clutch master cylinder. Clean and replace parts as necessary. Refit. Check and adjust brakes as necessary.	2 1
2599	Remove off-side front door furniture and drop glass. Beat out and reshape off-side front door. Fit new drop glass. Flat down off-side front door and blend to rear wing. Prime and prepare. Respray in colour. Fit new parts as listed below. Refit all removed parts.	10

| JOB COST CARD | | | | | | | | | | | | | | Job No. | | |

Customer — Customer's Order No. — Vehicle make

Job Description

Estimate Ref. — Invoice No. — Vehicle reg. no.

Quoted price — **Invoice price** — Date to collect

Material						Labour								Overheads			
Date	Req. No.	Qty.	Price	Cost		Date	Emp-loyee	Cost Ctre	Hrs.	Rate	Bonus	Cost		Hrs	OAR	Cost	
				£	p							£	p			£	p
Total C/F						Total C/F								Total C/F			

Expenses						Job Cost Summary	Actual		Estimate	
							£	p	£	p
Date	Ref.	Description	Cost							
			£	p		Direct Materials B/F				
						Direct Expenses B/F				
						Direct Labour B/F				
						Direct Cost				
						Overheads B/F				
						Admin overhead (add 10%)				
						= Total Cost				
						Invoice Price				
Total C/F						Job Profit/Loss				

Comments

Job Cost Card Completed by ....

JOB COST CARD

Customer		Customer's Order No.	Vehicle make
Job Description			
Estimate Ref.		Invoice No.	Vehicle reg. no.
Quoted price		Invoice price	Date to collect

Job No.

Material						Labour								Overheads			
Date	Req. No.	Qty.	Price	Cost		Date	Emp-loyee	Cost Ctre	Hrs.	Rate	Bonus	Cost		Hrs	OAR	Cost	
				£	p							£	p			£	p
Total C/F						Total C/F								Total C/F			

Expenses						Job Cost Summary	Actual		Estimate	
							£	p	£	p
Date	Ref.	Description	Cost							
			£	p		Direct Materials B/F				
						Direct Expenses B/F				
						Direct Labour B/F				
						Direct Cost				
						Overheads B/F				
						Admin overhead (add 10%)				
						= Total Cost				
						Invoice Price				
Total C/F						Job Profit/Loss				

Comments

Job Cost Card Completed by ....

JOB COST CARD

		Job No.
Customer	Customer's Order No.	Vehicle make
Job Description		
Estimate Ref.	Invoice No.	Vehicle reg. no.
Quoted price	Invoice price	Date to collect

Material						Labour								Overheads			
Date	Req. No.	Qty.	Price	Cost		Date	Emp-loyee	Cost Ctre	Hrs.	Rate	Bonus	Cost		Hrs	OAR	Cost	
				£	p							£	p			£	p
Total C/F						Total C/F								Total C/F			

Expenses						Job Cost Summary	Actual		Estimate	
							£	p	£	p
Date	Ref.	Description	Cost							
			£	p		Direct Materials B/F				
						Direct Expenses B/F				
						Direct Labour B/F				
						Direct Cost				
						Overheads B/F				
						Admin overhead (add 10%)				
						= Total Cost				
						Invoice Price				
Total C/F						Job Profit/Loss				

Comments

Job Cost Card Completed by ....

JOB COST CARD

	Job No.
Customer	Customer's Order No.	Vehicle make
Job Description		Vehicle reg. no.
Estimate Ref.	Invoice No.	
Quoted price	Invoice price	Date to collect

Material						Labour								Overheads			
Date	Req. No.	Qty.	Price	Cost		Date	Emp-loyee	Cost Ctre	Hrs.	Rate	Bonus	Cost		Hrs	OAR	Cost	
				£	p							£	p			£	p
Total C/F						Total C/F								Total C/F			

Expenses					Job Cost Summary	Actual		Estimate	
						£	p	£	p
Date	Ref.	Description	Cost						
			£	p	Direct Materials B/F				
					Direct Expenses B/F				
					Direct Labour B/F				
					Direct Cost				
					Overheads B/F				
					Admin overhead (add 10%)				
					= Total Cost				
					Invoice Price				
Total C/F					Job Profit/Loss				

Comments

Job Cost Card Completed by ....

JOB CARD				A926
Customer	Mrs Crankley			
Vehicle	Metro			
Reg. no.	A 987 OPB			
Estimate ref.	2583 and 2589			
Name	John Moore/Tony Booth			
Employee ref.	012/007			
Date commenced	11.6.X3/12.6.X3			

WORK DONE	MINS	ON	OFF
Examine distributor, centre bearing and ascertain reason for knocking		11.15 14.00	12.00 15.15
Work agreed and done by Tony:			
Dismantle distributor, replace parts and reassemble		08.15	09.27
Ditto commutator end frame		09.27	10.50
Realign centre bearing		10.55	11.30
TOTAL (or c/fwd)			

JOB CARD				A930
Customer	Mr F Jenkins			
Vehicle	Sierra			
Reg. no.	F109 HEV			
Estimate ref.	2594			
Name	Ed Murray			
Employee ref.	009			
Date commenced	13.6.X3			

WORK DONE	MINS	ON	OFF
Remove clutch master cylinder		09.15	09.45
Dismantle and inspect for wear		09.45	10.25
Replace parts as necessary and refit		12.00	12.30
Check brakes and adjust as necessary		14.45	15.32
TOTAL (or c/fwd)			

JOB CARD				B638
Customer	Mr Robert			
Vehicle	TR7			
Reg. no.	RGY 367W			
Estimate ref.	2574			
Name	Dave Bishop			
Employee ref.	016			
Date commenced	13.6.X3			

WORK DONE	MINS	ON	OFF
Remove damaged vent and fit new vent		9.11	11.00
Mask up and spray etc		11.15	12.00
Spray 2nd coat		14.37	15.03
Remove masking and finish off		15.30	16.15
TOTAL (or c/fwd)			

JOB CARD				B641
Customer	Mr J White			
Vehicle	Peugeot 205 GTi			
Reg. no.	G 614 SOX			
Estimate ref.	2599			
Name	Jeff Wilson			
Employee ref.	018			
Date commenced	12.6.X3			

WORK DONE	MINS	ON	OFF
Remove off-side front door furniture and drop glass		08.00	09.47
		15.25	15.37
Beat out and reshape off-side front door			
		09.24	11.31
Fit new drop glass. Flat down off-side front door and blend to rear wing		11.07	12.58
Prime and prepare. Respray in colour			
Fit new parts and refit removed parts		14.10	16.07
TOTAL (or c/fwd)			

```
  ○   ISSUE NOTE    36807                12:06:X3              08:30      ○
  ○                                                                      ○
  ○     QTY             PART NO.             UNIT COST         TOTAL COST ○
  ○                                                                      ○
  ○      1             T265347               7.18               7.18     ○
  ○                                                                      ○
  ○                            DISRIBUTOR CLAMP                          ○
  ○            JOB: A926                          REF: 007               ○
```

```
  ○   ISSUE NOTE    36808                12:06:X3              08:31      ○
  ○                                                                      ○
  ○     QTY             PART NO.             UNIT COST         TOTAL COST ○
  ○                                                                      ○
  ○      2             T386434               1.24               2.48     ○
  ○                                                                      ○
  ○                            SPRING CLIP                               ○
  ○            JOB: A926                          REF: 007               ○
```

```
  ○   ISSUE NOTE    36815                12:06:X3              08:40      ○
  ○                                                                      ○
  ○     QTY             PART NO.             UNIT COST         TOTAL COST ○
  ○                                                                      ○
  ○      1             T68111                75.49              75.49     ○
  ○                                                                      ○
  ○                            DROP GLASS                                ○
  ○            JOB: B641                          REF: 018               ○
```

```
  ○   ISSUE NOTE    36816                12:06:X3              08:41      ○
  ○                                                                      ○
  ○     QTY             PART NO.             UNIT COST         TOTAL COST ○
  ○                                                                      ○
  ○      1             T75710                33.19              33.19     ○
  ○                                                                      ○
  ○                            MOULDING                                  ○
  ○            JOB: B641                          REF: 018               ○
```

```
  ○   ISSUE NOTE    36821                12:06:X3              09:38      ○
  ○                                                                      ○
  ○     QTY             PART NO.             UNIT COST         TOTAL COST ○
  ○                                                                      ○
  ○      1             T839849               88.40              88.40     ○
  ○                                                                      ○
  ○                            FIELD COIL                                ○
  ○            JOB: A926                          REF: 007               ○
```

```
ISSUE NOTE   36830              12:06:X3              11.05

QTY          PART NO.              UNIT COST        TOTAL COST

1            T437105                 61.90             61.90

                      CENTRE BEARING

             JOB: A926                    REF: 007
```

```
ISSUE NOTE   36842              12:06:X3              15:27

QTY          PART NO.              UNIT COST        TOTAL COST

5            T057897                  6.01             30.05

                       BODY FILLER

             JOB: B641                    REF: 018
```

```
ISSUE NOTE   36861              13:06:X3              09:58

QTY          PART NO.              UNIT COST        TOTAL COST

1            T999636                 45.20             45.20

                     PUSHROD CLEVIS

             JOB: A930                    REF: 009
```

```
ISSUE NOTE   36867              13:06:X3              10:14

QTY          PART NO.              UNIT COST        TOTAL COST

1            T62908                  72.56             72.56

                          VENT

             JOB: B638                    REF: 016
```

```
ISSUE NOTE   36868              13:06:X3              10:15

QTY          PART NO.              UNIT COST        TOTAL COST

1            T765354                  3.03              3.03

                    VENT FITTINGS PACK

             JOB: B638                    REF: 016
```

```
ISSUE NOTE   36874              13:06:X3              10:20

QTY            PART NO.             UNIT COST       TOTAL COST

 1             T759251               6.95             6.95

                       HOLE SNAP RING

        JOB: A930                      REF: 009
```

```
ISSUE NOTE   36881              13:06:X3              11:20

QTY            PART NO.             UNIT COST       TOTAL COST

 5             T889388               3.99             19,95

                        RED PAINT

        JOB: B641                      REF: 018
```

```
ISSUE NOTE   36885              13:06:X3              12:04

QTY            PART NO.             UNIT COST       TOTAL COST

 1             T680538               8.75             8.75

                     COMPRESSION SPRING

        JOB: A930                      REF: 009
```

```
ISSUE NOTE   36894              13:06:X3              14.38

QTY            PART NO.             UNIT COST       TOTAL COST

 3             T889386               3.99             11.97

                        BLUE PAINT

        JOB: B638                      REF: 016
```

```
ISSUE NOTE   36902              13:06:X3              15:02

QTY            PART NO.             UNIT COST       TOTAL COST

 2             T498204               35.80            71.60

                        BRAKE SHOE

        JOB: A930                      REF: 009
```

NORMAN JOLLEY

"Expert panel beating"
47 Thump Street, Little Wallop, LW14 9QT

To/

2 hours work on
Peugeot 205 GTI   50.00

50.00

Received with thanks   Norm

PAYROLL SUMMARY - W/E 9.6.X3

NAME	NO.	BASIC	BONUS	TOTAL	PAYE	EMPLOYEE NI	OTHER DEDS	NET	EMPLOYER NI
COST CENTRE A									
BOOTH, A	007	240.00	15.00	255.00	46.17	22.95	5.00	180.88	26.65
DUNCAN, R	008	260.00	30.00	290.00	54.60	24.94	-	210.46	30.17
MURRAY, E	009	260.00	24.00	284.00	52.95	24.50	10.00	196.55	29.65
BOOTH, T	010	280.00	-	280.00	49.35	24.36	-	206.29	29.23
LINCOLN, T	011	280.00	-	280.00	48.36	24.36	-	207.28	29.23
MOORE, J	012	280.00	19.50	299.50	59.20	26.05	10.00	204.25	31.27
COST CENTRE B									
BISHOP, D	016	240.00	13.00	253.00	39.50	20.24	-	193.26	26.41
SMITH, P	017	280.00	-	280.00	49.35	24.36	-	206.29	29.23
WILSON, J	018	260.00	20.00	280.00	47.50	24.36	-	208.14	29.23
		2,380.00	121.50	2,501.50	446.98	216.12	25.00	1,813.40	261.07

Practice devolved assessment
3 *Strange (Properties) Ltd*

Performance criteria

The following performance criteria are covered in this Devolved Assessment.

Element 5.1: Record and analyse information relating to direct costs

1   Direct costs are identified in accordance with the organisation's costing procedures

2   Information relating to direct costs is clearly and correctly coded, analysed and recorded

3   Direct costs are calculated in accordance with the organisation's policies and procedures

6   Queries are either resolved or referred to the appropriate person

Element 5.2: Record and analyse information relating to the allocation, apportionment and absorption of overhead costs

1   Data are correctly coded, analysed and recorded

2   Overhead costs are established in accordance with the organisation's procedures

3   Information relating to overhead costs is accurately and clearly recorded

4   Overhead costs are correctly attributed to producing and service cost centres in accordance with agreed methods of allocation, apportionment and absorption

5   Adjustments for under or over recovered overhead costs are made in accordance with established procedures

7   Methods of allocation, apportionment and absorption are revised at regular intervals in discussion with senior staff and agreed changes to methods implemented

8   Staff working in operational departments are consulted to resolve any queries in the data

Notes on completing the Assessment

This Assessment is designed to test your ability to operate and maintain a system of accounting for expenses and a system for the apportionment and absorption of indirect costs.

You are provided with data on Pages 230 to 241 which you must use to complete the tasks on Pages 238 and 241.

You are allowed **three hours** to complete your work.

A high level of accuracy is required. Check your work carefully.

Correcting fluid should not be used. Errors should be crossed out neatly and clearly. You should write in ink - not pencil.

A full suggested solution to this Assessment is provided on Page 315.

Do not turn to the suggested solution until you have completed all parts of the Assessment.

PRACTICE DEVOLVED ASSESSMENT 3: STRANGE (PROPERTIES) LTD

Data

Your name is John Vernon and you joined Strange (Properties) Ltd at the beginning of November, taking over as head of the accounts department on the retirement of Brian Dimple who had occupied the post for many years.

Strange (Properties) Ltd is a property management company headed by Edward Strange, a solicitor, and his brother Victor, a chartered surveyor. The company looks after all of the affairs of around thirty blocks of flats or estates in the surrounding area. This involves company secretarial services, conveyancing, dealing with disputes, regular inspections of sites, obtaining tenders for repairs and maintenance contracts, bookkeeping, cash management and so on - a huge variety of tasks in fact.

During your first month you have spent most of your time chasing debtors, since there are many long-outstanding debts and a large bank overdraft as a consequence. You have left the day to day cash management to your two assistants. However, you have just received the following memo and attachments from Edward Strange.

MEMO

To: John Vernon
From: Edward Strange
Date: 1 December 19X2
Subject: Charges to clients

A number of our clients have complained recently about the way our charges fluctuate from month to month. Have you seen this list that the auditors did for July to September? I vaguely remember that your predecessor, Brian Dimple, used to say something about costing, and things not balancing, and fictional whatnots, but this was in the days before we bought the computer. Perhaps things are different now.

I was talking to an accountant at the golf club the other night and he started on about various different sorts of costing. 'Standard costing' was mentioned and 'absorbent costing'. One I thought might be appropriate to Strange (Properties) was 'process costing': I've heard you talk about processing invoices and data processing and the like.

Could you have a think about this and let me have a suggestion. I'll grin and bear it if 'notional thingummies' really are too bothersome, but I would like to appease our uppity paymasters if it does no harm to our business.

Enc. List of client charges; letter to Loudwater Place, copy invoices.

<table>
<tr><td colspan="4" align="center">***Client charges***
July to September 19X2</td></tr>
<tr><td></td><td align="center">*July*
£</td><td align="center">*August*
£</td><td align="center">*September*
£</td></tr>
<tr><td>Ashby Mansions, Harlington</td><td>2,336</td><td>2,705</td><td>2,220</td></tr>
<tr><td>Burgess Court, Southall</td><td>2,580</td><td>3,425</td><td>2,716</td></tr>
<tr><td>Clerk Court, Ealing</td><td>3,112</td><td>2,913</td><td>2,580</td></tr>
<tr><td>Clift Flats, Heston</td><td>2,656</td><td>3,233</td><td>2,959</td></tr>
<tr><td>Clifton Gardens, Hounslow</td><td>2,761</td><td>2,705</td><td>2,875</td></tr>
<tr><td>Coomer Place, Putney</td><td>2,730</td><td>2,705</td><td>2,142</td></tr>
<tr><td>Davison Close, Acton</td><td>2,200</td><td>3,215</td><td>2,330</td></tr>
<tr><td>De Beauvoir Buildings, Chiswick</td><td>2,807</td><td>4,171</td><td>2,975</td></tr>
<tr><td>Endymion Place, Hammersmith</td><td>3,230</td><td>2,705</td><td>2,721</td></tr>
<tr><td>Frampton Court, Fulham</td><td>5,185</td><td>3,429</td><td>2,142</td></tr>
<tr><td>Gibbs House, Hounslow</td><td>2,586</td><td>2,847</td><td>2,850</td></tr>
<tr><td>Glebe Gardens, Perivale</td><td>2,200</td><td>2,705</td><td>2,455</td></tr>
<tr><td>Grasmere Mansion, Isleworth</td><td>2,943</td><td>3,131</td><td>2,142</td></tr>
<tr><td>Hennigan House, Wembley</td><td>2,544</td><td>3,482</td><td>2,562</td></tr>
<tr><td>Jones Court, Fulham</td><td>2,338</td><td>2,705</td><td>5,740</td></tr>
<tr><td>Ketley Close, Sheen</td><td>6,905</td><td>2,705</td><td>3,909</td></tr>
<tr><td>Kings Buildings, Petersham</td><td>2,596</td><td>2,962</td><td>2,462</td></tr>
<tr><td>Laine House, Hanwell</td><td>2,806</td><td>2,765</td><td>2,804</td></tr>
<tr><td>Loudwater Place, Kew</td><td>2,200</td><td>8,983</td><td>3,858</td></tr>
<tr><td>Matkins Gardens, Hounslow</td><td>2,751</td><td>2,910</td><td>2,142</td></tr>
<tr><td>Mallow Close, Ealing</td><td>2,531</td><td>3,554</td><td>2,458</td></tr>
<tr><td>Neville House, Acton</td><td>3,463</td><td>2,961</td><td>2,791</td></tr>
<tr><td>Oakwood Buildings, Roehampton</td><td>2,580</td><td>2,864</td><td>2,304</td></tr>
<tr><td>Queen's Court, Isleworth</td><td>2,479</td><td>2,705</td><td>3,102</td></tr>
<tr><td>Rhodes Close, Sheen</td><td>3,177</td><td>3,655</td><td>2,142</td></tr>
<tr><td>Rodway House, Chiswick</td><td>2,200</td><td>3,023</td><td>2,284</td></tr>
<tr><td>Seymour Manor, Hammersmith</td><td>2,891</td><td>2,705</td><td>2,538</td></tr>
<tr><td>Tilbury Tower, Wembley</td><td>3,448</td><td>2,846</td><td>2,403</td></tr>
<tr><td>Undercliff Gardens, Richmond</td><td>2,652</td><td>2,917</td><td>3,392</td></tr>
<tr><td>Wyndham Rise, Southall</td><td>2,549</td><td>3,454</td><td>2,142</td></tr>
</table>

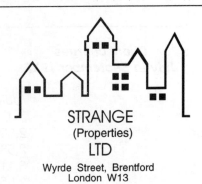

STRANGE
(Properties)
LTD

Wyrde Street, Brentford
London W13

Peter Purviss
17, Loudwater Place
Kew
London

1 December 19X2

Dear Peter,

<u>Monthly Fees</u>

Thank you for your letter of 24 November.

I note what you say about your cash flow and your difficulty in knowing what level of service charges to set your fellow residents. Indeed, this is a matter of concern to us too especially where we (in theory) hold cash on behalf of our clients. I have already instructed our staff to look into our costing procedures to see if anything can be done and I am hoping that a solution that is not too much of an administrative burden can be arrived at.

With best wishes for Christmas and the New Year

Yours sincerely

Edward

E. Strange

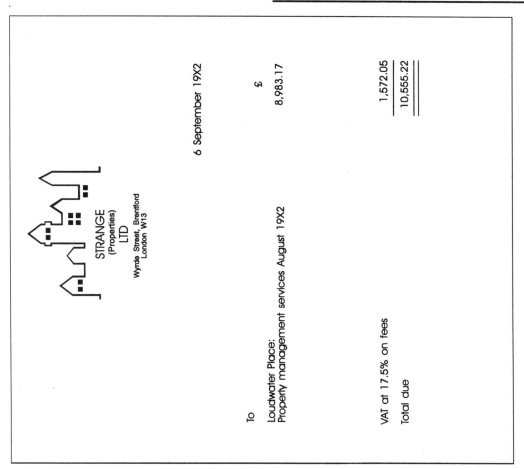

STRANGE
(Properties)
LTD
Wyrde Street, Brentford
London W13

6 September 19X2

To

Loudwater Place:
Property management services August 19X2

£

8,983.17

VAT at 17.5% on fees

1,572.05

Total due

10,555.22

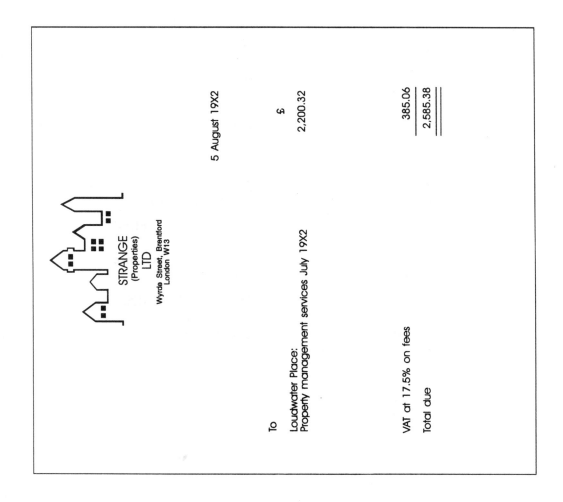

STRANGE
(Properties)
LTD
Wyrde Street, Brentford
London W13

5 August 19X2

To

Loudwater Place:
Property management services July 19X2

£

2,200.32

VAT at 17.5% on fees

385.06

Total due

2,585.38

You are aware that clients' monthly charges are made up as follows.

	£
Direct expenses paid by Strange (Properties) Ltd	X
Fixed fee	1,500.00
One-thirtieth share of overheads incurred in the month	X
	X

The treatment of overheads seems reasonable as far as your own department's services are concerned, because you and your staff do indeed seem to spend a roughly equal amount of time on each client. However you are not sure how fair it is with respect to other work.

In any case you decide to see what the charges for November will be on this basis. You have the cash book for November but this has not yet been coded up for posting. You also have a list of account codes.

Account codes

Range	Sub-account	Name
100		STAFF COSTS
	/001	Wages
	/002	Salaries
	/003	PAYE and NI
	/010	Staff welfare
	/020	Employer's liability insurance
200		TRAVEL COSTS
	/001	Petrol
	/002	Motor insurance
	/003	Fares and taxis
300		BUILDINGS COSTS
	/001	Heat and light
	/002	Buildings insurance
	/003	Rates
	/004	Repairs and maintenance
	/005	Cleaning
400		COMMUNICATIONS
	/001	Postage
	/002	Telephone
	/003	Stationery
	/004	Computer sundries
500		PROFESSIONAL FEES
	/001	Auditors
	/002	Public liability insurance
	/003	Subscriptions
600		FINANCE CHARGES
	/001	Bank interest
	/002	Bank charges

Range	Sub-account	Name
700		PUBLICITY
	/001	Advertising
	/002	Entertaining
800		CLIENT CODES
	/001	Rodway House
	/100	Matkins Gardens
	/101	Glebe Gardens
	/105	Gibbs House
	/110	Grasmere Mansion
	/189	Seymour Manor
	/225	Queen's Court
	/250	Loudwater Place
	/261	De Beauvoir Buildings
	/274	Jones Court
	/301	Ashby Mansions
	/325	Kings Buildings
	/350	Clift Flats
	/376	Neville House
	/401	Frampton Court
	/429	Hennigan House
	/430	Wyndham Rise
	/450	Coomer Place
	/501	Laine House
	/525	Undercliff Gardens
	/555	Burgess Court
	/556	Ketley Close
	/605	Mallow Close
	/620	Clifton Gardens
	/675	Endymion Place
	/750	Oakwood Buildings
	/801	Davison Close
	/890	Tilbury Tower
	/914	Rhodes Close
	/999	Clerk Court
900		SUNDRIES
	/001	E S expenses
	/002	V S expenses
	/003	General sundries

No.	Date	Description	Code	Total
	November			
1	1	Caretaker - Clerk Court		76.50
2	1	Sankey Builders, Sheen - Ketley		600.00
3	1	Post Office		3.61
4	1	Sundries - Gibbs Ho		52.80
5	1	Perivale Glass Co.		317.00
6	3	Motor Mower - Burgess Ct		263.00
7	4	Electricity - Ketley Cl, (to 28,10)		355.84
8	4	Water rates - Q.C		92.00
9	4	Inst, Ch, Surveyors		515.00
10	5	Hanwell DIY		69.10
11	8	Law Society (subs)		742.00
12	8	Inland Revenue		8,437.50
13	8	Gas - Mallow Cl, (to 5.11)		81.50
14	9	Cleaners - Seymour M.		390.01
15	10	Power Drill - Laine Ho.		48.90
16	13	Perivale Roofing		4,720.00
17	17	Dentone (sols) - re Ashby M.		723.37
18	17	Coomer PL - Caretaker		226.00
19	17	Kew Electrics		590.72
20	17	Southern Electricity (to 15.11)		1,110.43
21	17	Wyrde St Computer Supplies		33.00
22	18	Brentford Advertiser		66.50
23	19	Rentokil - Jones Co.		856.06
24	21	Nevill Ho - Skip Hire (17.10-19.11)		32.40
25	21	Hanwell Timber		236.00
26	21	Sankeys - Ketley Clo.		1,800.00
27	24	Heston Service Station		8.81
28	24	Bldgs Ins - Oakwood B		408.00
29	24	Plumbing Supplies (Petersham) Ltd - Kings		426.80
30	24	Wages - Grasmere Caretaker		279.19
31	25	BACS - Salaries		12,187.89
32	25	British Gas - Tilbury		35.60

No.	Date	Description	Code	Total
	November			
1	26	Hall Hire - Wyndham AGM		32.50
2	26	Sainsbury's		19.50
3	28	Caretaker - Rodway Ho.		438.00
4	28	Property Management News		18.40
5	28	British Telecom		475.70
6	28	Co. House - Wyndham		32.00
7	28	Concrete repairs - Tilbury T		2,250.00
8	28	Acton Skip Hire - 1.11-30.11 - Davison		32.40
9	28	Brentford Cleaning		183.00
10	28	Wages - Davison Clo. C/T		66.10
11	28	Wages - Endymion Pl. C/T		64.50
12	28	Middlesex Gazette		22.22
13	28	Ben Smith Stationery Supplies		178.57
14	28	Electricity - Hennigan Ho. (to 25.11)		568.35
15	28	Guardian Royal Exchange - Pub. Liab		970.00
16	28	Guardian Royal Exchange - Richm.. Bldgs		1,630.00
17	28	E Strange Exps		88.90
18	28	Non-Dom Rates DD		271.25
19	28	GRE - Jaguar		1,315.50
20	28	Bank - charges		70.90
21	28	Bank - interest		949.93
22				
23				
24				
25				
26				
27				
28				
29				
30				
31				
32				

Tasks

Task 1

(a) Code up the entries in the cash book, allocating the payments either directly to clients or to the appropriate Strange (Properties) Ltd account.

   (*Note.* You can assume that geographical references in a cash book entry mean that the cost should be allocated to the buildings in the same location.)

(b) Prepare a schedule of client charges using the current basis for allocating charges. Ignore VAT for the purposes of this part of the exercise.

If any matters occur to you at this stage for your reply to Mr Strange's memo, make rough notes. (You will be writing your reply later.)

Task 2

Amongst the debtors you have been pursuing are five former clients who dispensed with Strange (Properties) Ltd's services earlier in the year. The telephone conversations and letters that you have had have contained comments like 'I don't see why we should subsidise your business!'; 'You do next to nothing for us as far as we know'; 'Why are we paying for building works on your other clients' properties?' and so on.

You decide to see if you can find a way of charging each client a fair proportion of the overheads incurred and to do this you collect or compile the following materials:

(a) A rough plan of the building

(b) An organisation chart

(c) A copy of Strange (Properties) Ltd's accounts for the year ended 30 September 19X2

(d) A summary of the timesheets of Edward Strange and Victor Strange for the year 19X1/19X2

These documents, or extracts from them, are shown below.

Floor plan

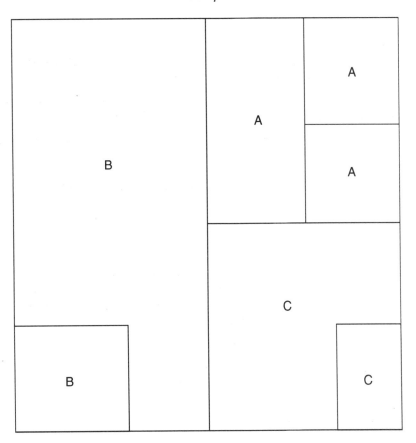

A = Solicitors staff
B = Surveying staff
C = Accounts staff

Organisation chart

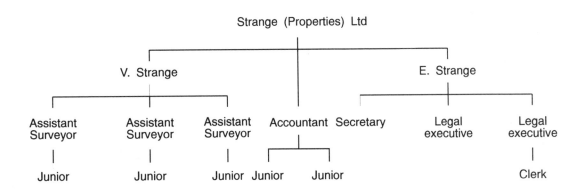

STRANGE (PROPERTIES) LTD
PROFIT AND LOSS ACCOUNT FOR THE YEAR ENDED
30 SEPTEMBER 19X2

	£	£
Fees		1,333,838
Less direct expenses		352,187
		981,651
Less costs of administration		
Wages and salaries	272,255	
Business rates	3,524	
Insurance	7,600	
Heat and light	4,775	
Depreciation of motor vehicles	7,500	
Depreciation of office equipment	1,752	
Repairs and maintenance	834	
Cleaning	6,584	
Depreciation of buildings	4,000	
Staff welfare	1,538	
Telecommunications	1,908	
Printing, postage and stationery	3,975	
Subscriptions	1,131	
Audit and accountancy fees	4,500	
Bank charges	862	
Advertising	1,973	
		324,711
		656,940
Interest payable		10,121
Profit before tax		646,819
Taxation		159,680
Profit for the financial year		487,139
Dividends		475,320
Retained profit transferred to reserves		11,819

STRANGE (PROPERTIES) LTD
BALANCE SHEET AS AT 30 SEPTEMBER 19X2

Fixed assets	*Leased buildings* £	*Motor vehicles* £	*Office equipment* £	*Total* £
Cost	80,000	30,000	17,520	127,520
Depreciation	48,000	22,500	7,008	77,508
	32,000	7,500	10,512	50,012
Current assets				
Debtors			309,060	
Prepayments			5,296	
			314,356	
Creditors				
Bank overdraft		113,880		
Other creditors		47,294		
Dividends		50,000		
			211,174	
				103,182
				153,194
Share capital				20,000
Profit and loss account				133,194
				153,194

(*Note.* The motor vehicles are the two second-hand Jaguars used by the Strange brothers. Both cost £15,000.)

TIME SHEET SUMMARY 19X1/X2

Current clients	Edward Strange Hours	Victor Strange Hours
Ashby Mansions	43	20
Burgess Court	71	82
Clerk Court	62	34
Clift Flats	15	113
Clifton Gardens	25	64
Coomer Place	60	80
Davison Close	49	52
De Beauvoir Buildings	74	38
Endymion Place	33	51
Frampton Court	16	73
Gibbs House	51	21
Glebe Gardens	81	60
Grasmere Mansion	84	30
Hennigan House	76	94
Jones Court	61	66
Ketley Close	49	36
Kings Buildings	63	57
Laine House	45	77
Loudwater Place	73	48
Matkins Gardens	76	35
Mallow Close	57	61
Neville House	24	92
Oakwood Buildings	117	40
Queen's Court	51	18

	Edward Strange *Hours*	*Victor Strange* *Hours*
Rhodes Close	82	97
Rodway House	64	88
Seymour Manor	23	64
Tilbury Tower	29	59
Undercliff Gardens	80	71
Wyndham Rise	75	28

Ex-clients		
Anderson Place	14	8
Jacques Court	25	12
Oxford Gardens	22	14
Robin House	20	15
Williams Close	30	22

Your task is to apportion the administrative and selling expenses and interest shown in the accounts as you think appropriate and to calculate how much should have been charged to each of Strange (Properties) Ltd's current clients.

Task 3

Reply to Mr Strange's memo, offering a solution to his problem. You may, of course, give him a copy of the calculations that you have already done. It would also be helpful to explain to him briefly about different methods of costing, but bear in mind that he has a very limited understanding of accountancy jargon.

Practice devolved assessment
4 Valerie Andrews

Performance criteria

The following performance criteria are covered in this Devolved Assessment.

Element 5.1: Record and analyse information relating to direct costs

4   Standard costs are compared against actual costs and any variances are analysed

Element 5.2: Record and analyse information relating to the allocation, apportionment and absorption of overhead costs

6   Standard costs are compared against actual costs and any variances are analysed

Element 5.3: Prepare and present standard cost reports

1   Standard cost reports with variances clearly identified are presented in an intelligible form

2   Unusual or unexpected results are identifed and reported to managers

3   Any reasons for significant variances from standard are identified and the explanations presented to management

4   The results of the analysis and explanations of specific variances are produced for management

5   Staff working in operational departments are consulted to resolve any queries in the data

Notes on completing the Assessment

This Assessment is designed to test your ability to prepare and present standard cost reports.

You are provided with data on Pages 244 to 246 which you must use to complete the tasks on Pages 244 to 246.

You are allowed **three hours** to complete your work.

A high level of accuracy is required. Check your work carefully.

Correcting fluid should not be used. Errors should be crossed out neatly and clearly. You should write in ink - not pencil.

A full suggested solution to this Assessment is provided on Page 323.

Do not turn to the suggested solution until you have completed all parts of the Assessment.

SECTION 1

PRACTICE DEVOLVED ASSESSMENT 4: VALERIE ANDREWS

Data

You work as the assistant to the management accountant for a major hotel chain, Stately Hotels plc. The new manager of one of the largest hotels in the chain, The Regent Hotel, is experimenting with the use of standard costing to plan and control the costs of preparing and cleaning the hotel bedrooms.

Two of the costs involved in this activity are cleaning labour and the supply of presentation soap packs.

Cleaning labour

Part-time staff are employed to clean and prepare the bedrooms for customers. The employees are paid for the number of hours that they work, which fluctuates on a daily basis depending on how many rooms need to be prepared each day.

The employees are paid a standard hourly rate for weekday work and a higher hourly rate at the weekend. The standard cost control system is based on an average of these two rates at £3.60 per hour.

The standard time allowed for cleaning and preparing a bedroom is fifteen minutes.

Presentation soap packs

A presentation soap pack is left in each room every night. The packs contain soap, bubble bath, shower gel, hand lotion etc. Most customers use the packs or take them home with them, but many do not. The standard usage of packs used for planning and control purposes is one pack per room per night.

The packs are purchased from a number of different suppliers and the standard price is £1.20 per pack. Stocks of packs are valued in the accounts at standard price.

Actual results for May

During May, 8,400 rooms were cleaned and prepared. The following data was recorded for cleaning labour and soap packs.

Cleaning labour paid for:

Weekday labour	1,850	hours @ £3 per hour
Weekend labour	700	hours @ £4.50 per hour
	2,550	

Presentation soap packs purchased and used:

6,530	packs @ £1.20 each	
920	packs @ £1.30 each	
1,130	packs @ £1.40 each	
8,580		

Tasks

1   Using the data above, calculate the following cost variances for May:

    (a)   Soap pack price
    (b)   Soap pack usage
    (c)   Cleaning labour rate
    (d)   Cleaning labour utilisation or efficiency

2   Suggest one possible cause for each of the variances which you have calculated.

SECTION 2

Data

You are employed as the assistant management accountant to Albion Ltd. Albion Ltd manufactures a single product, the Xtra, an ingredient used in food processing. The basic raw material in Xtra production is material X. The average unit prices for material X in each quarter last year are reproduced below.

	Quarter 1	*Quarter 2*	*Quarter 3*	*Quarter 4*
Average unit price of X	£10	£11	£16	£19

Albion Ltd operates a standard absorption costing system. Standards are established at the beginning of each year. Each week the management accounting section prepares a statement for the production director reconciling the actual cost of production with its standard cost. Standard costing data for week 8 of quarter 4 in the current year is given below.

Standard costing and budget data for week 8 of quarter 4			
	Quantity	*Unit price*	*Cost per unit*
Material (kilograms)	3	£23.00	£69
Labour (hours)	2	£20.00	£40
Fixed overheads (hours)	2	£60.00	£120
Standard unit cost			£229
Budgeted production for week 8	*Budgeted units*	*Standard cost per unit*	*Standard cost of production*
	10,000	£229	£2,290,000

During week 8, production of Xtra totalled 9,000 units and the actual costs for that week were:

Inputs	*Units*	*Total cost*
Materials (kilograms)	26,500	£662,500
Labour (hours)	18,400	£349,600
Fixed overheads (hours)	18,400	£1,500,000

Using this data, a colleague has already calculated the fixed overhead variances. These were as follows:

- Fixed overhead expenditure (or price) variance   £300,000 adverse
- Efficiency (or usage) variance   £24,000 adverse
- Capacity variance   £96,000 adverse

Tasks

Your colleague asks you to:

1   Calculate the following variances:

    (a)   material price;
    (b)   material usage;
    (c)   labour rate;
    (d)   labour efficiency (sometimes called utilisation).

2   Prepare a statement listing all of the cost variances.

SECTION 3

Data

You are employed as part of the management accounting team in a large industrial company which operates a four-weekly system of management reporting. Your division makes a single product, the Alpha, and, because of the nature of the production process, there is no work in progress at any time.

The group management accountant has completed the calculation of the material and labour standard costing variances for the current period to 1 December but has not had the time to complete any other variances. Details of the variances already calculated are produced in the working papers below, along with other standard costing data.

Standard costing and budget data - four weeks ended 1 December			
	Quantity	*Unit price*	*Cost per unit*
Material (litres)	40	£4.00	£160
Labour (hours)	10	£8.40	£84
Fixed overheads (hours)	10	£6.70	£67
Standard cost per unit			£311
	Units	*Standard unit cost*	*Standard cost of production*
Budgeted production	12,000	£311	£3,732,000

Working papers:

Actual production and expenditure for the four weeks ended 1 December

Units produced	11,200
Cost of 470,000 litres of materials consumed	£1,974,000
Cost of 110,000 labour hours worked	£935,000
Expenditure on fixed overheads	£824,000

Material and labour variances

Material price variance	£94,000	(A)
Materials usage variance	£88,000	(A)
Labour rate variance	£11,000	(A)
Labour efficiency variance	£16,800	(F)

Tasks

1   Calculate the following variances.

   (a)   The fixed overhead expenditure variance
   (b)   The fixed overhead volume variance
   (c)   The fixed overhead capacity variance
   (d)   The fixed overhead efficiency variance

2   Prepare a report for presentation to the production director showing the cost variances for the 4 weeks ended 1 December.

3   The production director, who has only recently been appointed, is unfamiliar with fixed overhead variances. Because of this, the group management accountant has asked you to prepare a *brief* memo to the production director.

   Your memo should do the following:

   (a)   Explain what is meant by fixed overhead expenditure, volume, capacity and efficiency variances.

   (b)   Suggest one possible cause for each of the variances that you have calculated.

Trial run devolved assessment

TRIAL RUN DEVOLVED ASSESSMENT

INTERMEDIATE STAGE - NVQ/SVQ3

Unit 5

Recording cost information

The purpose of this Trial Run Devolved Assessment is to give you an idea of what a Devolved Assessment could be like. It is not intended as a definitive guide to the tasks you may be required to perform.

The suggested time allowance for this Assessment is two and a half hours.

Calculators may be used but no reference material is permitted.

**DO NOT OPEN THIS PAPER UNTIL YOU ARE READY TO START
UNDER TIMED CONDITIONS**

INSTRUCTIONS

This Assessment is designed to test your ability to record cost information.

Background information is provided on Page 251.

The tasks you are to perform are set out on Page 252.

You are provided with data on Pages 253 to 266 which you must use to complete the tasks.

Your answers should be set out in the answer booklet on Pages 267 to 275 using the documents provided. You may require additional answer pages.

You are allowed **four hours** to complete your work.

A high level of accuracy is required. Check your work carefully.

Correcting fluid may not be used. Errors should be crossed out neatly and clearly. You should write in black ink, not pencil.

You are advised to read the whole of the Assessment before commencing as all of the information may be of value and is not necessarily supplied in the sequence in which you might wish to deal with it.

A full suggested solution to this Assessment is provided on Pages 327 to 334.

THE SITUATION

It is your first day at your new job. You should have started as the accountant at Food with a Bite Ltd four weeks ago (1 March 19X3), the company's first day of business. A broken leg from a rather nasty fall on the Matterhorn during a skiing holiday has, however, delayed your joining the company.

You arrive on Monday 29 March knowing that you have four weeks work to catch up on but nobody seems to be around the factory or offices apart from Fred and Ali, the two production line workers. They explain that their supervisor is dealing with a delivery, the storeman won't be starting for another week (his wife has had a baby and so Harry Jordan, the General Manager, has given him five weeks paternity leave) and that Harry Jordan himself is out of the office for the day. All that you need has, however, been left on your desk, which they point you in the direction of.

On your desk you find three piles of documents marked financial accounts, management accounts and cost accounts and a note from Harry Jordan.

It seems as if you are going to have to cope on your own for the day and you quickly try to assemble in your mind all that you know about Food with a Bite Ltd from your conversations with Harry Jordan at your interviews.

(a) The company began trading on 1 March 19X3.

(b) It makes two products, a hot vegetarian chilli in the chilli production department and a spicy vegetarian curry in the curry production department.

(c) Two production line workers are employed. Ali is initially working on the chilli production line and Fred is initially working on the curry production line. Eventually they will both work on either production line as demand dictates. They are overseen by a supervisor. A storekeeper (when he finally begins working) will look after the stores area (the company's other department). He will spend half of his time controlling the chilli ingredients and half of his time controlling the curry ingredients.

(d) The company's year is divided into 13 four-week periods.

(e) There is a great demand for the two products. Sam's Supermarkets have agreed to take (on a Friday) whatever has been produced during the week.

You pick up Harry's note.

Friday 26 March

Sorry to leave you in the lurch! Hope I've left everything you're going to need on your desk.
Can you start with cost accounting because I desperately need your help for the board meeting on Friday. I've got to take standard cost cards for our two products with me and give them some idea about how efficiently Fred has been working over the last four weeks. The board also want to know how efficiently he's been using the vegetables in the curry.
Do you think you can prepare the cards (I don't know what they are but the board gave me a couple of blanks) and find out about Fred and the vegetables? The board also expect to see updated stores ledger accounts (whatever they are) for lentils and vegetables. Again, they've given me a couple of blanks.
Thanks very much. See you on Wednesday.

Harry

TASKS TO BE COMPLETED

In the answer booklet on Pages 267 to 275 complete the tasks outlined below. Data for this assessment is provided on Pages 253 to 266.

As you complete each of the tasks you should note any matters which need discussing with members of staff on a schedule of queries indicating who you will need to speak to and any action which may be necessary. You should ignore VAT and employer's National Insurance contributions and work to two decimal places.

(a) Calculate standard material costs for a vegetarian chilli and a vegetarian curry, basing the standard quantities on the information provided by Delia Craddock and the standard prices on the expected prices at 1 September 19X3. (Materials includes cartons.)

Fill in the details of the standard quantities and standard prices, and hence the standard material costs, on each of the standard cost cards.

(b) Calculate standard labour costs for a vegetarian chilli and a vegetarian curry using information from the business plan and the offers of employment.

Fill in the details of the standard times and standard wage rates, and hence the standard labour costs, on each of the standard cost cards.

(c) Calculate standard variable overhead costs for a vegetarian chilli and a vegetarian curry using information provided by Oly from Oly's Oils.

Fill in the details of the standard quantity and standard price, and hence the standard overhead cost, on each of the standard cost cards.

(d) (i)   Calculate the budgeted annual fixed overheads, fixed overheads being the salaries of the supervisor and storekeeper, the cost of cleaners, heat and light and overtime.

(ii)   Allocate (if possible) overheads direct to departments.

(iii)   Apportion the remaining overheads between the three departments using suitable bases (budgeted direct labour hours, floor area and overtime hours).

(iv)   Apportion the service department overheads to the two production departments.

(v)   Calculate departmental overhead absorption rates based on direct labour hours.

Fill in the details of the standard overhead absorbed into each product on the standard cost card. You should now have two completed standard cost cards.

(e) Calculate a labour efficiency variance for the curry department for the four-week period using details from the clock cards and standard cost cards and the fact that 5,000 portions of curry were made.

(f) Complete (as fully as possible, given the available information) stores ledger accounts for the four-week period for lentils and vegetables using the information provided in the list of what was taken from the storeroom and the two Exotic Foods Emporium invoices. Use the stock valuation method recommended in the business plan.

(g) Calculate a usage variance for the vegetables used during the four-week period using information on the appropriate stores ledger account and standard cost card.

(h) Calculate any under- or over-absorption of fixed overhead during the four-week period. To determine the overtime cost incurred you need to know, in addition to the information you already have, that 5,300 portions of chilli were made and that Ali worked 171.25 hours.

DATA

(a) The following letter and list of ingredients were received from Delia Craddock.

```
Mr H. Jordan                        Apple Cottage
Food With a Bite Ltd                Rose Lane
Spicy Court                         Little Smedlingford
Riceford


                                    23rd February 19X3


Dear Harry

What a lovely surprise hearing from  you after so many years.
Yes, of course I remember our days at Univesity together. How
could I forget!! Do you remember that poem you recited to me as
we punted down the river?

I'm so pleased your business empire is expanding and I'd love to
help in any way I can. I enclose a list of the standard
ingredients for vegetarian chilli and vegetarian curry. I hope
it's what you needed.

I look forward to seeing you on the 29th March. I'll be in
black!

Enc.

           Delia

        Delia Craddock
```

```
Standard ingredients for one portion
Vegetarian chilli
0.125 kg rice
0.0625 kg lentils
0.167 kg tinned tomatoes
0.167 kg mushroom/onion/pepper mixture
0.167 kg kidney beans
0.025 kg dried chillis
0.167 kg vegetables

Vegetarian curry
0.125 kg rice
0.167 litres coconut oil
0.005 kg spices
0.167 kg vegetables
```

(b) The following compliments slip and current price list were received from Exotic Foods Emporium.

xotic Foods Emporium

Please find enclosed current price list. As to your enquiry, our prices have increased by 10% since 1.3.X2. It is likely that our prices will increase by a similar percentage during the coming

With Compliments

xotic Foods Emporium
The Industrial Estate
Riceford
0321 909 698

PRICE LIST at 1.3.X3

		£
Chillis - 50 kg drum	95.15	86.50
Coconut oil - 100 l drum	126.50	115.00
Kidney beans - 50 kg drum	48.40	44.00
Lentils - 100 kg sack	92.40	84.00
Mushroom/onion/pepper - 50 kg drum	63.80	58.00
Rice - 100 kg sack	143.	130.00
Spices - 10 kg drum	101.20	92.00
Tomatoes - 50 kg drum	38.50	35.00
Vegetables - 50 kg drum	58.85	53.50

(c) The following quotation was received from a carton manufacturer.

 The Container Company   Matfield Road   Riceford

QUOTATION

25/2/X3

Plastic food containers (1 portion) with appropriate design on cardboard lid: unit price 4p.

Price increase to 5p from 1.4.X3. Fixed for 12 months.

(d) The following extract from the Business Plan for Food With a Bite Ltd was prepared by Smethick & Co (Management Consultants).

Extracts from Business Plan
for
Food with a Bite Ltd
by
Smethick & Co
(Management Consultants)

Expected production for 12 months (13 periods) to 28.2.X4

Vegetarian chilli - 78,000 portions
Vegetarian curry - 66,300 portions

Expected labour time to produce 1 portion

Vegetarian chilli - 1.5 minutes
Vegetarian curry - 2 minutes

Per discussion with National Electricity

Likely charge per annum for heat and light £5,000

Recommendations

Initially, value issues and stock using weighted average method. Standard costing will be used once the company and its operations are established.

Asborb overheads on basis of direct labour hours.

Do not allow annual overtime to exceed 100 hours in total for both production line workers. Overtime should not be regular occurrence once system established.

(e)   The following offers of employment were sent out in the middle of February.

Food with a Bite
Spicy Court
Riceford

Mr A Khan   20 February 19X3
132 The Drive
Riceford

Dear Mr Khan

I have great pleasure in offering you the position of
production line worker (chilli) at Food with a Bite.

Your basic rate of pay will be £4.00 per hour. Any hours
worked over and above the basic time of eight hours a day
will be paid at time and a half. During your first year of
service you are entitled to one day's holiday. This will be
increased to four weeks in your second year of service.

I look forward to hearing from you in the very near future.

Yours sincerely

Harry Jordan

Harry Jordan

Food with a Bite

Spicy Court
Riceford

Mr F Jarvis   20 February 19X3
44 The Close
Riceford

Dear Mr Jarvis

I have great pleasure in offering you the position of
production line worker (curry) at Food with a Bite.

Your basic rate of pay will be £4.00 per hour. Any hours
worked over and above the basic time of eight hours a day
will be paid at time and a half. During your first year of
employment you are entitled to one day's holiday. This will
be increased to four weeks in your second year of service.

I look forward to hearing from you in the very near future.

Yours sincerely

Harry Jordan

Harry Jordan

Food with a Bite

Spicy Court
Riceford

Mr J Simpson   20 February 19X3
4 The Street
Riceford

Dear Mr Simpson

I have great pleasure in offering you the position of
production line supervisor at Food with a Bite.

Your starting salary will be £16,000 per annum with an annual
review on 1 April 19X4 and every April thereafter. You are
entitled to four weeks' holiday per annum.

I look forward to hearing from you in the very near future.

Yours sincerely

Harry Jordan

Harry Jordan

Food with a Bite

Spicy Court
Riceford

Mr K Sampson   20 February 19X3
2 The Road
Riceford

Dear Mr Sampson

I have great pleasure in offering you the position of
Storekeeper at Food with a Bite.

Your starting salary will be £12,000 per annum with an annual
review on 1 April 19X4 and every April thereafter. You are
entitled to four weeks' holiday per annum.

I look forward to hearing from you in the very near future.

Yours sincerely

Harry Jordan

Harry Jordan

(f)   The following telephone message was taken on the 15th March 19X3.

Telephone Message

Mr Jordan

while you were out

Oly from Oly's Oils ....called

at .... 9.00 .... on .... 15/3/X3 ....

Message ....

line machines @ £17.50 per 10 litre drum. Said to tell you

price hasn't changed for last 4 years and unlikely to in

future. You'll probably need to use 1 litre of oil per

machine for every 100 portions produced by machine.

(g)   The following contract is for cleaning the factory and stores of Food With a Bite Ltd.

Mrs Mopp Cleaners

Contract

With:

Food with a Bite Ltd
Spicy Court
Riceford

From: 1/3/X3

To: 28/2/X4

For: 2 hours cleaning per night
             (factory and stores areas)

At: £10 per hour

For Mrs Mopp Cleaners: V. Rix   (Director)

For: Food with a Bite Ltd   N. Richards   (Director)

(h) The following floor plan shows the factory and stores area.

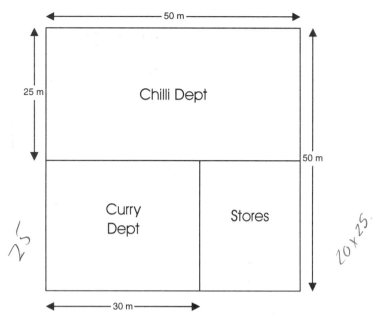

(i) The following electricity bill was received at the end of March 19X3.

NATIONAL ELECTRICITY

YOUR CUSTOMER SERVICES OFFICE IS:	YOU CAN PHONE US ON:
POWER ROAD RICEFORD	0321 949 494

FOOD WITH A BITE LTD
SPICY COURT
RICEFORD

WHEN TELEPHONING
We have a call queuing system. When you hear the ringing tone please wait for a reply as calls are answered in strict rotation.
BUSY TIMES
Please try to avoid 9-30AM - 10-30 AM and 2 PM to 3 PM

METER READING		UNITS USED	UNIT PRICE (pence)	V.A.T code	AMOUNT £
PRESENT	PREVIOUS				
2359 E	-	2359	17.470	1	412.12
STANDING CHARGE				1	217.50
TOTAL CHARGE (EXCLUDING VAT)					629.62
VAT 1 629.62 @ 17.5% COMMERCIAL					110.18

MAKE YOUR BILLS EASIER TO SWALLOW - SEE PAGE 4 OF 'SOURCE' FOR BUDGET SCHEME APPLICATION

E=Estimated reading. Please read carefully the advice given on the back of this bill
C=Your own reading

BALANCE TO PAY	739.80
VAT CHARGE THIS BILL	110.18

YOUR ACCOUNT NUMBER	BILL DATE/TAX POINT	READING DATE	NON-DOMESTIC USE
34721193672	26.03.X3	26.03.X3	100%

(j) The following four clock cards cover the weeks ending 5 March 19X3 and 12 March 19X3.

No _101_			Ending _5/3/X3_

Name *Fred Jarvis*

	HOURS	RATE	AMOUNT	DEDUCTIONS	
Basic	38			Income Tax	
O/T	1			NI	
Others				Other	
				Total deduction	
Total					
Less deductions					
Net due					

Time	Day	Basic time	Overtime
1630	F		
1330	F	3	
1230	F	4½ 7½	
0800	F		
1700	T		
1330	T	3½ 7½	
1230	T	4	
0830	T		
1830	W ✓		
1330	W	4 8	1
1300	W ✓	5	
0800	W		
1700	T ✓		
1330	T	3½ 7½	
1230	T ✓	4	
0830	T		
1700	M ✓		
1330	M ✓	3½ 7½	
1230	M ✓	4	
0830	M		

Signature ....

No _101_			Ending _12/3/X3_

Name *Fred Jarvis*

	HOURS	RATE	AMOUNT	DEDUCTIONS	
Basic	39			Income Tax	
O/T	1			NI	
Others				Other	
				Total deduction	
Total					
Less deductions					
Net due					

Time	Day	Basic time	Overtime
1630	F		
1330	F	3 7	
1200	F	4	
0800	F		
1800	T ✓		
1330	T	4½ 8	1
1230	T ✓	4½	
0800	T		
1630	W		
1330	W	3 8	
1230	W ✓	5	
0730	W		
1630	T ✓		
1330	T	3 8	
1230	T ✓	5	
0730	T		
1630	M ✓		
1330	M	3 8	
1230	M ✓	5	
0730	M		

Signature ....

Card 1

No	*101*		Ending	*5/3/X3*

Name *Fred Jarvis*

	HOURS	RATE	AMOUNT	DEDUCTIONS	
Basic	38			Income Tax	
O/T	2			NI	
Others				Other	
				Total deduction	

Total	
Less deductions	
Net due	

Time	Day	Basic time	Overtime
1630	F	3	
1330	F		
1230	F	4½ 7½	
0800	F		
1700	T ✓	3½ 7½	
1330	T		
1230	T ✓	4	
0830	T		
1830	W ✓	5	
1330	W ✓	8	2
1300	W ✓	5	
0800	W		
1700	T	3½ 7½	
1330	T ✓		
1230	T ✓	4	
0830	T		
1700	M ✓	3½ 7½	
1330	M		
1230	M ✓	4	
0830	M ✓		

Signature ....

Card 2

No	*101*		Ending	*12/3/X3*

Name *Fred Jarvis*

	HOURS	RATE	AMOUNT	DEDUCTIONS	
Basic	39			Income Tax	
O/T	1			NI	
Others				Other	
				Total deduction	

Total	
Less deductions	
Net due	

Time	Day	Basic time	Overtime
1630	F	2 7	
1330	F		
1200	F ✓	4	
0800	F		
1800	T ✓	4½ 8	1
1330	T		
1230	T ✓	4½	
0800	T		
1630	W	3	
1330	W ✓		
1230	W ✓	5 8	
0730	W		
1630	T ✓	3	
1330	T	8	
1230	T ✓	5	
0730	T		
1630	M ✓	3	
1330	M		
1230	M ✓	5 8	
0730	M		

Signature ....

(k)   The following list shows what Fred and Ali took from stores.

○ ○

What we took from storeroom

Mon 1 March
- 1 sack/drum of each food stuff
- 2,000 cartons

Wed 3 March
- 2 rice
- 3 toms
- 3 mush
- 3 kidney
- 2,000 cartons
- 1 coconut
- 3 veg

Mon 8 March
- 5 veg
- 5 rice
- 1 lentil
- 5 toms
- 5 mush
- 5 kidney
- 3,000 cartons
- 2 coconut
- 1 spice

Mon 15 March
- 2 rice
- 1 lentil
- 4 toms
- 4 mush
- 4 kidneys
- 2,000 cartons
- 2 coconut
- 1 spice
- 4 veg
- 1 chilli

Mon 22 March
- 3 rice
- 1 lentil
- 1 chilli
- 5 toms
- 5 kidney
- 5 mush
- 3,000 cartons
- 3 coconut
- 5 veg

Fri 26 March
no stock left in production
line area

Whenever we took rice or cartons, I had half
for chilli and Fred took half for curry

---

(1) The following two invoices were received from Exotic Foods Emporium.

---

xotic Foods Emporium
The Industrial Estate
Riceford
0321 909 698

Food with a Bite Ltd
Spicy Court
Riceford

INVOICE

Order no: 0001   Del date: 1/3/X3   Invoice no: 7164   Date: 1/3/X3

Quantity	Description	Unit price £	Total £
10	Rice - 100 kg sack	130.00	1,300.00
4	Lentils - 100 kg sack	84.00	336.00
10	Tomatoes - 50 kg drum	35.00	350.00
10	Mushs etc - 50 kg drum	58.00	580.00
10	Vegetables - 50 kg drum	53.50	535.00
6	Coconut oil - 100 l drum	115.00	690.00
3	Spice - 10 kg tin	92.00	276.00
10	Kidney beans - 50 kg drum	44.00	440.00
2	Chillis - 50 kg drum	86.50	173.00
		Total	4,680.00

This agrees with what was delivered
Fred Jarvis
1/3/X3

xotic Foods Emporium
The Industrial Estate
Riceford
0321 909 698

Food with a Bite Ltd
Spicy Court
Riceford

INVOICE

Order no: 003   Del date: 12/3/X3 Invoice no: 7321   Date: 12/3/X3

Quantity	Description	Unit price £	Total £
4	Rice - 100 kg sack	131.00	524.00
10	Tomatoes - 50 kg drum	35.00	350.00
10	Mushs etc - 50 kg drum	58.50	585.00
11	Vegetables - 50 kg drum	53.75	591.25
4	Coconut oil - 100 l drum	118.00	472.00
12	Kidney beans - 50 kg drum	44.00	528.00
3	Chillis - 50 kg drum	86.50	259.50
		Total	3,309.75

*Only 2 drums of chillis delivered
but 5 sacks of rice came
Fred Jarus
12/3/X3*

TRIAL RUN DEVOLVED ASSESSMENT

Recording Cost Information

ANSWER BOOKLET

Documents for use in this Assessment

The documents you will need to prepare the solution are given on Pages 269 to 271 and consist of two blank standard cost cards and two blank stores ledger accounts. Pages 272 to 275 are blank and can be used for any written solutions, calculations or workings.

Standard cost cards

STANDARD COST CARD

PRODUCT ....

DESCRIPTION	QUANTITY	COST PER KG/HOUR/ETC	EXTENSION	TOTAL
Materials		£	£	£
SUB-TOTAL				
Labour				
SUB-TOTAL				
Direct cost				
Variable o/h				
Standard variable cost				
Fixed o/h				
Standard cost of sale				

STANDARD COST CARD

PRODUCT ....

DESCRIPTION	QUANTITY	COST PER KG/HOUR/ETC	EXTENSION	TOTAL
Materials		£	£	£
SUB-TOTAL				
Labour				
SUB-TOTAL				
Direct cost				
Variable o/h				
Standard variable cost				
Fixed o/h				
Standard cost of sale				

Stores ledger accounts

STORES LEDGER ACCOUNT

Material: ....   Maximum Quantity: ....

Code: ....   Minimum Quantity: ....

Date	Receipts				Issues				Stock		
	G.R.N. No.	Quantity	Unit Price £	Amount £	Stores Req. No.	Quantity	Unit Price £	Amount £	Quantity	Unit Price £	Amount £

STORES LEDGER ACCOUNT

Material: ....   Maximum Quantity: ....

Code: ....   Minimum Quantity: ....

Date	Receipts				Issues				Stock		
	G.R.N. No.	Quantity	Unit Price £	Amount £	Stores Req. No.	Quantity	Unit Price £	Amount £	Quantity	Unit Price £	Amount £

Blank 1

Blank 2

Blank 3

Blank 4

Solutions for Unit 5

SOLUTIONS TO SAMPLE SIMULATION

DO NOT TURN THIS PAGE UNTIL YOU HAVE
COMPLETED THE SAMPLE SIMULATION

SOLUTIONS TO SAMPLE SIMULATION: POLYCOT LTD

Task 1

STORES LEDGER ACCOUNT

Material description: *Plastic poppers, boxes of 100*

Code no: *PP29*

Maximum quantity: *180*
Minimum quantity: *62*
Reorder level: *95*
Reorder quantity: *100*

Date	Receipts			Issues			Stock balance		
	Quantity	Price per box £	Total £	Quantity	Price per box £	Total £	Quantity	Price per box £	Total £
1 March							75	62.50	4,687.50
2 March	100	63.70	6,370.00				75	62.50	4,687.50
							100	63.70	6,370.00
							175		11,057.50
6 March				75	62.50	4,687.50			
				15	63.70	955.50			
				90		5,643.00	85	63.70	5,414.50
9 March	100	64.40	6,440.00				85	63.70	5,414.50
							100	64.40	6,440.00
							185		11,854.50
12 March	100	66.50	6,650.00				85	63.70	5,414.50
							100	64.40	6,440.00
							100	66.50	6,650.00
							285		18,504.50
20 March				85	63.70	5,414.50	75	64.40	4,830.00
				25	64.40	1,610.00	100	66.50	6,650.00
				110		7,024.50	175		11,480.00

STORES LEDGER ACCOUNT

Material description: *Cotton, 50m rolls*

Code no: *C733*

Maximum quantity:	*175*	
Minimum quantity:	*55*	
Reorder level:	*75*	
Reorder quantity:	*90*	

Date	Receipts			Issues			Stock balance		
	Quantity	Price per roll £	Total £	Quantity	Price per roll £	Total £	Quantity	Price per roll £	Total £
1 March							65	85.50	5,557.50
6 March	90	86.80	7,812.00				65	85.50	5,557.50
							90	86.80	7,812.00
							155		13,369.50
10 March				50	85.50	4,275.00	15	85.50	1,282.50
							90	86.80	7,812.00
							105		9,094.50
12 March	90	88.20	7,938.00				15	85.50	1,282.50
							90	86.80	7,812.00
							90	88.20	7,938.00
							195		17,032.50
18 March				15	85.50	1,282.50	65	86.80	5,642.00
				25	86.80	2,170.00	90	88.20	7,938.00
				40		3,452.50	155		13,580.00
30 March				30	86.80	2,604.00	35	86.80	3,038.00
							90	88.20	7,938.00
							125		10,976.00

Task 2

MEMO

To: Patrick McGrath
From: Lesley Hunt
Date: 3 April 1998
Subject: Stock levels during March

During March the stock levels of both plastic poppers (PP29) and 50 metre cotton rolls exceeded their maximum levels.

In the case of the cotton, stock of 195 rolls was held between 12 March and 18 March (maximum level: 175 rolls).

In the case of the plastic poppers, the maximum level is 180 boxes but this was exceeded on 9 March when a new delivery brought stocks up to 185. The situation became worse on 12 March when a delivery of a further 100 boxes was received. Clearly we should never have placed this additional order: the usual reorder level is 95 boxes.

I recommend that in future we should institute more thorough checks before orders are placed with suppliers and in particular a check to ensure that the reorder level has been reached.

Task 3

TIMESHEET

Week ending   *6 March 1998*

Employee name   *Amy Harding*   **Employee number**   *2173*

Department   *Finishing*   **Employee grade**   *2*

Activity	Monday Hours	Tuesday Hours	Wednes-day Hours	Thursday Hours	Friday Hours	Total Hours
Machining	*7*	*10*	*4*		*4*	*25*
Holiday			*4*	*8*		*12*
Waiting for work	*1*					*1*
Training					*4*	*4*
Total hours payable for day	*8*	*10*	*8*	*8*	*8*	*42*
Number of covers produced	*65*	*72*	*30*	*0*	*32*	
Bonus payable @ £0.15 per cover above 60 per day	*£0.75*	*£1.80*	*-*	*-*	*-*	*£2.55*

Signed   *Amy Harding*   **Manager**   *Jim Stubbs*

Analysis for week	Hours	Rate per hour £	Wages cost £
Direct wages	*25*	*3.00*	*75.00*
Indirect wages			
Basic hours	*17*	*3.00*	*51.00*
Overtime premium	*1*	*3.00*	*3.00*
Bonus	*-*	*-*	*2.55*
	43		*131.55*

TIMESHEET

Week ending   *6 March 1998*

Employee name   *Jane Amber*   **Employee number**   *2487*

Department   *Cutting*   **Employee grade**   *1*

Activity	Monday Hours	Tuesday Hours	Wednes-day Hours	Thursday Hours	Friday Hours	Total Hours
Cutting	*10*	*6*	*6*		*8*	*30*
Waiting for work		*3*	*2*			*5*
Sick				*8*		*8*
Training					*2*	*2*
Discrepancy		*(1)*				*(1)*
Total hours payable for day	*10*	*8*	*8*	*8*	*10*	*44*
Number of covers produced	*70*	*51*	*62*	*0*	*62*	
Bonus payable @ £0.15 per cover above 60 per day	*£1.50*	*-*	*£0.30*	*-*	*£0.30*	*£2.10*

Signed   *Jane Amber*   **Manager**   *Jim Stubbs*

Analysis for week	Hours	Rate per hour £	Wages cost £
Direct wages	*29*	*4.00*	*116.00*
Indirect wages			
Basic hours	*15*	*4.00*	*60.00*
Overtime premium	*2*	*4.00*	*8.00*
Bonus	*-*	*-*	*2.10*
	46		*186.10*

COST LEDGER DATA ENTRY SHEET

Week ending   *6 March 1998*

Debit accounts

	Cost centre code	Expenditure code	Amount to be debited £
	C100	E300	116.00
	C200	E300	75.00
	C300	E300	-
	C400	E300	-
	C100	E310	70.10
	C200	E310	56.55
	C300	E310	-
	C400	E310	-
Check total: total wages for the two employees			317.65

Task 4

MEMO

To: Jim Stubbs
From: Lesley Hunt
Date: 10 March 1998
Subject: Discrepancy on timesheet

I have a query on an employee's timesheet for the week ending 6 March 1998. The employee in question is Jane Amber, in the cutting department. A copy of the timesheet is enclosed.

You will see that I have had to adjust for a discrepancy of one hour. The total number of hours shown for Tuesday is eight, but the analysis totals to nine hours.

Could you please look into this for me? I have made the usual adjustments, pending the outcome of your enquires. Thanks for your help.

Task 5

MEMO

To: Jim Stubbs, production manager
From: Lesley Hunt, accounts assistant
Date: 10 March 1998
Subject: Standard rates for overhead absorption, 1998/99

Why the present absorption rate might not be the most appropriate for the company

The present system of absorbing production overheads using a percentage of direct labour cost may distort the overhead costs absorbed by individual products because of differential wage rates.

Our employees are paid different hourly rates. If a cost unit happens to be worked on by a highly paid employee its labour cost would be higher and the overhead absorbed would therefore also be higher. However the overhead actually incurred by this product would not necessarily be high, particularly if the higher paid employees work more quickly.

Many overhead costs tend to increase with time, for example rent, rates, salaries and so on. Therefore it makes sense to absorb overheads according to the time taken on a cost unit. Although a labour cost percentage is to an extent time based, it can lead to distortions when there are differential wage rates.

The hourly rates suggested would be preferable because the overhead absorbed would be directly related to the time taken to produce the cost unit.

Why separate hourly rates would be more suitable

The activity in the finishing and packing departments is labour intensive. Therefore a direct labour hour rate is most appropriate in these two departments. Using a separate rate for each department would more accurately reflect the load placed by a cost unit on the facilities of each department.

The cutting department is machine intensive. Therefore many of the overhead costs are likely to be machine related (for example depreciation and maintenance) and would be linked to the amount of time spent by a cost unit on the machines. Therefore a machine hour is more suitable in this department.

Task 6

OVERHEAD ANALYSIS SHEET: 1998/99

Overhead expense: primary apportionments and allocations	Basis of allocation/ apportionment	Total £	Cutting dept £	Finishing dept £	Packing dept £	Stores £
Rent and rates	Floor area	79,500	19,941	27,812	19,941	11,806
Catering	Number of employees	1,200	183	623	366	28
Machine maintenance	Quotation	45,850	25,250	5,600	11,000	4,000
Depreciation on machines	Cost of machines	13,490	7,412	1,663	3,230	1,185
Production manager's salary	Time spent	21,000	7,000	7,000	7,000	
Storekeeper's salary	Allocation	14,000				14,000
Other overheads	Even apportionment	40,000	10,000	10,000	10,000	10,000
Total of primary allocations		215,040	69,786	52,698	51,537	41,019
Re-apportion stores		_____	16,404	13,692	10,923	(41,019)
Total production cost						
centre overhead		215,040	86,190	66,390	62,460	
Machine hours			30,750			
Direct labour hours				129,750	67,500	
Overhead absorption rate for						
1998/99			£2.80	£0.51	£0.93	

Task 7a

MEMO

To: Jim Stubbs
From: Lesley Hunt
Date: 6 July 1998
Subject: Wages paid to temporary employee during the quarter ending 30 June 1998

I have been informed that £1,920 was paid to a temporary employee for 320 hours worked during the quarter ending 30 June 1998. To enable me to analyse and classify the hours worked by the employee and the wages paid, could you please provide me with the following information.

- How many of the 320 hours were worked on direct tasks, and how many were worked on indirect tasks? This will help me to determine the correct expenditure code for the wages payment.

- How many hours were worked in each of the three departments? This will help me to determine the correct cost centre code, and to complete the analysis of labour hours for the period.

Thank you for your help.

Working sheet for calculation of overhead under/over absorbed

Packing department, quarter ending 30 June 1998

7(b) Production overhead absorbed (using direct labour hour rate)	$18,300 \times £0.93$	£17,019
7(c) Actual production overhead incurred	$£855 + £4,045 + £10,800 + £800$	£16,500
7(d) Production overhead under or over absorbed, to be transferred to profit and loss account		£519 over absorbed

Task 8

STANDARD COST CARD 1998/99

Product: Box of 6 double duvet covers
Product code no: 00214

Description	Material code no/direct labour grade	Quantity	Std price £ per metre/ hour etc	Total £
Direct materials				
Cotton fabric	CT33	38.2 metres	1.85	70.67
Plastic poppers	PP29	60	0.67	40.20
Polyester thread	TP72	22 metres	0.00142	0.03
Packing - cardboard box	PB03	1 box	0.25	0.25
Other materials	Various	-	-	0.81
Subtotal, direct materials			(A)	111.96
Direct labour				
Cutting	Grade 1	0.35 hours	4.20	1.47
Finishing	Grade 1	4.10 hours	4.20	17.22
Packing	Grade 3	0.50 hours	2.63	1.31
Subtotal, direct labour			(B)	20.00
Production overhead				
Cutting department		1.80 machine hours	2.80	5.04
Finishing department		4.10 labour hours	0.51	2.09
Packing department		0.50 labour hours	0.93	0.46
Subtotal, production overhead			(C)	7.59
Total standard production cost			(A + B + C)	139.55

Task 9

MEMO

To: Patrick McGrath
From: Lesley Hunt
Date: 13 July 1998
Subject: Standard cost report - double duvet covers in Cutting department

As you requested, here is my interim report on the cost variances for week ended 8 July 1998.

	Favourable	*Adverse*
	£	£
Cotton price variance		568
Cotton usage variance		268
Direct labour rate variance		24
Direct labour efficiency variance	55	
Fixed overhead expenditure variance		54
Fixed overhead capacity variance		28
Fixed overhead efficiency variance	___	90
	£55	£1,032

Clearly the two variances that require investigation are those for usage and price of cotton. I will look into these as soon as possible, but likely explanations are as follows:

• We may have been unrealistic in setting our standards for price and usage.

• There may have been a recent price increase.

• We may have switched to a higher grade of cotton.

• Wastage levels may have increased.

Workings - variances for week ended 8/7/98 (cutting department)

	£
Cotton price variance	
11,350 metres should cost (@ £1.85)	20,997
did cost	21,565
Variance	568 (A)

	Metres
Cotton usage variance	
1,760 covers should require (@ 38.2/6)	11,205
did require	11,350
Difference	145
@ standard rate (£1.85)	£268 (A)

	£
Direct labour rate variance	
90 hours should cost (@ £4.20)	378
did cost	402
Variance	24 (A)

	Hours
Direct labour efficiency variance	
1,760 covers should require (@ 0.35/6)	103
did require	90
Difference	13
@ standard rate (£4.20)	£55 (F)

	£
Fixed overhead expenditure variance	
Budgeted overheads (1,900 × (1.8/6) × £2.80)	1,596
Actual overheads	1,650
Variance	54 (A)

	Hours
Fixed overhead capacity variance	
Budgeted hours worked (1,900 × 1.8/6)	570
Actual hours worked	560
Difference	10
@ standard rate (£2.80)	£28 (A)

	Hours
Fixed overhead efficiency variance	
Standard hours (1,760 × 1.8/6)	528
Actual hours	560
Difference	32
@ standard rate (£2.80)	£90 (A)

SOLUTION TO PRACTICE DEVOLVED ASSESSMENT 1: COUNTRY CUSTOM KITCHENS

Tutorial note. This is not a difficult assignment, but you could go hopelessly wrong if you don't keep your head and approach it in a methodical manner. It is vital that you study the cost accountant's note carefully before you start. Then see that you understand how the stock list is arranged and what the mass of figures mean.

Solution

(a)

STORES LEDGER ACCOUNT

Material: Supanut M4   Maximum Quantity: _____

Code: A1050   Minimum Quantity: _____

Date	Receipts				Issues				Stock		
	G.R.N. No.	Quantity	Unit Price £	Amount £	Stores Req. No.	Quantity	Unit Price £	Amount £	Quantity	Unit Price £	Amount £
Sept X3 6	b/f 24671	10	0.27	2.70					7 17	0.27 0.27	1.89 4.59

STORES LEDGER ACCOUNT

Material: Washer 30mm   Maximum Quantity: _____

Code: A2040   Minimum Quantity: _____

Date	Receipts				Issues				Stock		
	G.R.N. No.	Quantity	Unit Price £	Amount £	Stores Req. No.	Quantity	Unit Price £	Amount £	Quantity	Unit Price £	Amount £
Sept X3 6	b/f				0914	15	0.37	5.55	99 84	0.37 0.37	36.63 31.08

STORES LEDGER ACCOUNT

Material: ...... Roundhead screws 30mm ......   Maximum Quantity: ....

Code: ...... A4040 ......   Minimum Quantity: ....

Date	Receipts				Issues				Stock		
	G.R.N. No.	Quantity	Unit Price £	Amount £	Stores Req. No.	Quantity	Unit Price £	Amount £	Quantity	Unit Price £	Amount £
Sept X3 6	b/f				0915	10	0.28	2.80	13 3	0.28 0.28	3.64 0.84

STORES LEDGER ACCOUNT

Material: ...... Roundhead screws 40mm ......   Maximum Quantity: ....

Code: ...... A4060 ......   Minimum Quantity: ....

Date	Receipts				Issues				Stock		
	G.R.N. No.	Quantity	Unit Price £	Amount £	Stores Req. No.	Quantity	Unit Price £	Amount £	Quantity	Unit Price £	Amount £
Sept X3 6	b/f 24673	30	0.20	6.00					10 40	0.20 0.20	2.00 8.00

STORES LEDGER ACCOUNT

Material: Brass screw 45mm   Maximum Quantity: ....

Code: A6070   Minimum Quantity: ....

Date	Receipts				Issues				Stock		
	G.R.N. No.	Quantity	Unit Price £	Amount £	Stores Req. No.	Quantity	Unit Price £	Amount £	Quantity	Unit Price £	Amount £
Sept X3 6	b/f 24639	50	0.56	28.00					29 79	0.56 0.56	16.24 44.24

STORES LEDGER ACCOUNT

Material: Panel pins 35mm   Maximum Quantity: ....

Code: B2050   Minimum Quantity: ....

Date	Receipts				Issues				Stock		
	G.R.N. No.	Quantity	Unit Price £	Amount £	Stores Req. No.	Quantity	Unit Price £	Amount £	Quantity	Unit Price £	Amount £
Sept X3 6	b/f				0919	2	1.99	3.98	30 28	1.99 1.99	59.70 55.72

STORES LEDGER ACCOUNT

Material: ....Butt Hinge-chromium 40mm.......   Maximum Quantity: ....

Code: ....D0060.......   Minimum Quantity: ....

Date	Receipts				Issues				Stock		
	G.R.N. No.	Quantity	Unit Price £	Amount £	Stores Req. No.	Quantity	Unit Price £	Amount £	Quantity	Unit Price £	Amount £
Sept X3 6	b/f				0916	10	3.14	31.40	11 1	3.14 3.14	34.54 3.14

STORES LEDGER ACCOUNT

Material: ....Drawer runners.......   Maximum Quantity: ....

Code: ....F2010.......   Minimum Quantity: ....

Date	Receipts				Issues				Stock		
	G.R.N. No.	Quantity	Unit Price £	Amount £	Stores Req. No.	Quantity	Unit Price £	Amount £	Quantity	Unit Price £	Amount £
Sept X3 6	b/f				0917	8	2.49	19.92	122 114	2.49 2.49	303.78 283.86

STORES LEDGER ACCOUNT

Material: Lift off butt hinge - chromium 75mm

Code: D2080

Maximum Quantity:

Minimum Quantity:

Date	Receipts				Issues				Stock		
	G.R.N. No.	Quantity	Unit Price £	Amount £	Stores Req. No.	Quantity	Unit Price £	Amount £	Quantity	Unit Price £	Amount £
Sept X3	b/f								4	8.17	32.68
6	24638	10	8.17	81.70					14	8.17	114.38

STORES LEDGER ACCOUNT

Material: External Angle 19mm

Code: F2040

Maximum Quantity:

Minimum Quantity:

Date	Receipts				Issues				Stock		
	G.R.N. No.	Quantity	Unit Price £	Amount £	Stores Req. No.	Quantity	Unit Price £	Amount £	Quantity	Unit Price £	Amount £
Sept X3	b/f								113	1.99	224.87
6	24672	200	1.99	398.00					313	1.99	622.87

STORES LEDGER ACCOUNT

Material: .... Decorative Crowns ....   Maximum Quantity: ....

Code: .... F3070 ....   Minimum Quantity: ....

Date	Receipts				Issues				Stock		
	G.R.N. No.	Quantity	Unit Price £	Amount £	Stores Req. No.	Quantity	Unit Price £	Amount £	Quantity	Unit Price £	Amount £
Sept X3 6	b/f 24670	10	4.79	47.90					7 17	4.79 4.79	33.53 81.43

STORES LEDGER ACCOUNT

Material: .... Magnetic catch (white) ....   Maximum Quantity: ....

Code: .... F5010 ....   Minimum Quantity: ....

Date	Receipts				Issues				Stock		
	G.R.N. No.	Quantity	Unit Price £	Amount £	Stores Req. No.	Quantity	Unit Price £	Amount £	Quantity	Unit Price £	Amount £
Sept X3 6	b/f				0918	20	3.99	79.80	45 25	3.99 3.99	179.55 99.75

MATERIALS REQUISITION

Material Required for: *K309/93*
(Job or Overhead Account)

No. 0914

Date: *6.9.X3*

Quantity	Description	Code No.	Factor/ Unit	Rate	£	Notes
15	Steel washer 30mm	A2040	Pack 20	0.37	5.55	╱

Foreman: *Vlad Kopeii*   Costed and Coded: AAT

MATERIALS REQUISITION

Material Required for: *K309/93*
(Job or Overhead Account)

No. 0915

Date: *6.9.X3*

Quantity	Description	Code No.	Factor/ Unit	Rate	£	Notes
10	R/Hd 30mm	A4040	Pack 10	0.28	2.80	Reorder 10429

Foreman: *Vlad Kopeii*   Costed and Coded: AAT

MATERIALS REQUISITION

Material Required for: *K312/93*
(Job or Overhead Account)

No. 0916

Date: *6.9.X3*

Quantity	Description	Code No.	Factor/ Unit	Rate	£	Notes
10 chrome	Butt hinges 40mm	D0060	5 pairs	3.14	31.40	Reorder 10433

Foreman: *VK*   Costed and Coded: AAT

MATERIALS REQUISITION

Material Required for: *K313/93*
(Job or Overhead Account)

No. 0917

Date: *6.9.X3*

Quantity	Description	Code No.	Factor/ Unit	Rate	£	Notes
8	*Drawer runners*	F2010	1 pair	2.49	19.92	/

Foreman: *VK*   Costed and Coded: AAT

MATERIALS REQUISITION

Material Required for: *K313/93*
(Job or Overhead Account)

No. 0918

Date: *6.9.X3*

Quantity	Description	Code No.	Factor/ Unit	Rate	£	Notes
20	*White magnetic catches*	F5010	1	3.99	79.80	/

Foreman: *Vlad*   Costed and Coded: AAT

MATERIALS REQUISITION

Material Required for: *K309/93*
(Job or Overhead Account)

No. 0919

Date: *6.9.X3*

Quantity	Description	Code No.	Factor/ Unit	Rate	£	Notes
2	*Panel pins 35mm*	B2050	0.5kg	1.99	3.98	/

Foreman: *VK*   Costed and Coded: AAT

Tutorial note. Materials requisitions 0915 and 0916 relate to stock lines which are reordered (see purchase requisitions 10429 and 10433). Appropriate details (such as reorder number) are therefore included on the materials requisitions.

(b)   (i)   *Tutorial note.* As per the cost accountant's note, the reorder quantity is roughly one month's stock (to the nearest five) based on last year's figures.

		PURCHASE REQUISITION Req. No. 10427		
Department _Costing_			Date 6.9.X3	
Suggested Supplier: 28043112				
			Requested by: AAT	

Quantity	Code	Description	Estimated Cost	
			Unit	£
60	A2060	Brass washer 15mm	0.40	24.00

Authorised signature:

		PURCHASE REQUISITION Req. No. 10428		
Department _Costing_			Date 6.9.X3	
Suggested Supplier: 27561247				
			Requested by: AAT	

Quantity	Code	Description	Estimated Cost	
			Unit	£
50	A2070	Brass washer 20mm	0.45	22.50

Authorised signature:

PURCHASE REQUISITION   Req. No.   10429

Department ___Costing___

Suggested Supplier:

28043112

Date   6.9.X3

Requested by: AAT

Quantity	Code	Description	Estimated Cost	
			Unit	£
60	A4040	Roundhead screws 30mm	0.28	16.80

Authorised signature:

PURCHASE REQUISITION   Req. No.   10430

Department ___Costing___

Suggested Supplier:

23344248

Date   6.9.X3

Requested by: AAT

Quantity	Code	Description	Estimated Cost	
			Unit	£
65	A4080	Roundhead screws 50mm	0.28	18.20

Authorised signature:

PURCHASE REQUISITION   Req. No.   10431

Department ___Costing___   Date   6.9.X3
Suggested Supplier:
          21840027
                              Requested by: AAT

Quantity	Code	Description	Estimated Cost	
			Unit	£
15	D2030	Lift-off Butt hinge 65mm	4.58	68.70

Authorised signature:

PURCHASE REQUISITION   Req. No.   10432

Department ___Costing___   Date   6.9.X3
Suggested Supplier:
          28043112
                              Requested by: AAT

Quantity	Code	Description	Estimated Cost	
			Unit	£
1	F1070	Steel tube 25mm	7.07	7.07

Authorised signature:

```
┌─────────────────────────────────────────────────────────────────────────┐
│                    PURCHASE REQUISITION    Req. No.    10433              │
│                                                                           │
│   Department ___Costing_____            Date    6.9.X3                   │
│   Suggested Supplier:                                                      │
│            23344248                                                       │
│                                      Requested by:   AAT                   │
│                                                                           │
├──────────┬─────────┬──────────────────────────────┬──────────────────────┤
│          │         │                              │   Estimated  Cost    │
│ Quantity │  Code   │        Description           ├───────────┬──────────┤
│          │         │                              │   Unit    │    £     │
│          │         │                              │           │          │
│   10     │ D0060   │ Chromium Butt hinges 40mm    │   3.14    │  31.40   │
│          │         │                              │           │          │
├──────────┴─────────┴──────────────────────────────┴───────────┴──────────┤
│ Authorised signature:                                                     │
└─────────────────────────────────────────────────────────────────────────┘
```

Tutorial note. Requisition number 10433 relates to a stock line which was not highlighted as an exception on the stock report but the raising of materials requisition no 0916 means that there is only one item left in stock. Further hinges therefore need to be ordered.

(ii)   A copy of the purchase requisition (or better, the actual order) could be attached to the stock card until the order is received.

(c)

```
┌────────────────────────────────────────────────────────────────────────────┐
│                                                                              │
│  QUERY SCHEDULE                                                              │
│                                                                              │
│  Stock item       Query                                        Action        │
│                                                                              │
│  D0020            Nil stock but very slow-moving                             │
│                   Not re-ordered                                             │
│                                                                              │
│  D0030            As above                                                   │
│                                                                              │
│  D1020            As above                                                   │
│                                                                              │
│  D1030            As above                                                   │
│                                                                              │
│  F3080            As above                                                   │
│                                                                              │
│  F3090            As above                                                   │
│                                                                              │
│  F1020            As above, but appears to be identical to item F1030.       │
│                   Is this an error? (Current balance of F1030- 14 units,     │
│                   which is adequate on basis of previous period.)            │
│                                                                              │
│  B0010                                                                       │
│                                                                              │
│  B0020                                                                       │
│                                                                              │
│  B1010            These items are all very slow moving                       │
│                                                                              │
│  B1020                                                                       │
│                                                                              │
│  B1080                                                                       │
│                                                                              │
│  B1090                                                                       │
│                                                                              │
│  D0010            Very slow moving stock but 15 units delivered on 3         │
│                   September. Is this OK?                                     │
│                                                                              │
│  -                Invoice from Chippies Veneers- not a screw or fixing.      │
│                   Pass to whoever is dealing with panels stock.              │
│                                                                              │
│  -                Invoice 671493 from Higgins (27314295) includes 60         │
│                   'Screw Eyes' at £0.90. Stock list shows that 60 ×          │
│                   19mm screw eyes were on order at £0.76. 25mm               │
│                   screw eyes standard cost is £0.89. Has Higgins sent        │
│                   the wrong type? Have they been properly posted?            │
│                                                                              │
│  -                Are first few items in A section missing?                  │
│                                                                              │
│  -                What are stock items C and E?                              │
│                                                                              │
│  -                GRNs 24640 - 24669 missing, or 24670 and following         │
│                   used out of sequence.                                      │
│                                                                              │
└────────────────────────────────────────────────────────────────────────────┘
```

Tutorial note. Your query schedule may have contained many more points, especially if you had difficulty in finding any of the stock items or knowing how to post the entries. Our solutions to other parts of the assignment should clear up such queries: the important thing in practice is that you note down any matters that you are not sure about so that somebody can help you to resolve the problems later.

(d)

Journal No. _ _ _ _ _ _ _

Date	Customer/ supplier code	Invoice	Order No.	Stock code	Quantity	Net £	VAT (17.5%) £
03.09.X3	25567840	1187	2072	F0040	50	84 00	14 70
03.09.X3	25567840	1187	2072	F6080	4	8 28	1 45
03.09.X3	23344248	87161743	2178	A3020	15	3 60	0 63
03.09.X3	23344248	87161743	2178	A4070	75	18 00	3 15
03.09.X3	23344248	87161743	2178	A4090	40	14 00	2 45
03.09.X3	23344248	87161743	2178	A3050	80	28 00	4 90
03.09.X3	23344248	87161743	2178	B0030	10	27 20	4 76
03.09.X3	23344248	87161743	2178	F5050	40	198 00	34 65
03.09.X3	23344248	87161743	2178	D2070	10	62 00	10 85
03.09.X3	27314295	671493	2694	B2070	20	43 00	7 53
03.09.X3	27314295	671493	2694	B2050	30	59 70	10 45
03.09.X3	27314295	671493	2694	F3040	125	187 50	32 81
03.09.X3	27314295	671493	2694	F4080	60	54 00	9 45
03.09.X3	27314295	671493	2694	D3030	35	34 65	6 06
03.09.X3	27314295	671493	2694	B1070	60	179 40	31 40
03.09.X3	27314295	671493	2694	F1030	10	24 70	4 32

(e)

Stock code	Quantity	*Actual price* £	*Standard price* £	*Difference* £	*Variance* £
F0040	50	1.68	1.59	0.09	4.50
F6080	4	2.07	1.99	0.08	0.32
A3020	15	0.24	0.24	-	-
A4070	75	0.24	0.24	-	-
A4090	40	0.35	0.32	0.03	1.20
A3050	80	0.35	0.33	0.02	1.60
B0030	10	2.72	2.69	0.03	0.30
F5050	40	4.95	4.79	0.16	6.40
D2070	10	6.20	6.07	0.13	1.30
B2070	20	2.15	2.15	-	-
B2050	30	1.99	1.99	-	-
F3040	125	1.50	1.50	-	-
F4080	60	0.90	0.76	0.14	8.40
D3030	35	0.99	0.99	-	-
B1070	60	2.99	2.99	-	-
F1030	10	2.47	2.47	-	-
					24.02

(*Tutorial note.* Item F4080 is queried in (c) above. In practice the total variance could be calculated by comparing the total of materials purchases with the total value of receipts into stock, but this information is not available for this assignment.)

(f) See (c)

(g)

MRN	*Job* K309/93	*Job* K312/93	*Job* K313/93
0914	5.55		
0915	2.80		
0916		31.40	
0917			19.92
0918			79.80
0919	3.98		
	12.33	31.40	99.72

SOLUTION TO PRACTICE DEVOLVED ASSESSMENT 2: STANCOURT MOTORS

| JOB COST CARD | | | | | | | | | | | Job No. | B638 | | | |

Customer	Mr Robert		Customer's Order No.			Vehicle make	TR7
Job Description	Replace damaged vent					Vehicle reg. no.	RGY 367W
Estimate Ref. 2574			Invoice No.				
Quoted price	£159.56		Invoice price	£159.56		Date to collect	14.6.X3

Material						Labour								Overheads			
Date	Req. No.	Qty.	Price	Cost		Date	Emp-loyee	Cost Ctre	Hrs.	Rate	Bonus	Cost		Hrs	OAR	Cost	
				£	p							£	p			£	p
13.6	36867	1	72.56	72	56	13.6	016	B	3.75	6.00	1.50	24	00	3.75	2.50	9	38
13.6	36868	1	3.03	3	03												
13.6	36894	3	3.99	11	97												
Total C/F				87	56	Total C/F						24	00	Total C/F		9	38

Expenses						Job Cost Summary	Actual		Estimate	
							£	p	£	p
Date	Ref.	Description	Cost							
			£	p		Direct Materials B/F	87	56	87	56
						Direct Expenses B/F	-	-	-	-
						Direct Labour B/F	24	00	72	00
						Direct Cost	111	56		
						Overheads B/F	9	38		
							120	94		
						Admin overhead (add 10%)	12	09		
						= Total Cost	133	03	159	56
						Invoice Price	159	56		
Total C/F						Job Profit/Loss	26	53		

Comments

Job Cost Card Completed by ....

JOB COST CARD

Job No.	A926

Customer	Mrs Crankley	Customer's Order No.		Vehicle make	Metro

Job Description Distributor/Commutator

Estimate Ref. 2583/2589	Invoice No.	Vehicle reg. no.	A987 0PB

Quoted price	£249.96	Invoice price	£255.41	Date to collect	14.6.X3

Material						Labour								Overheads			
Date	Req. No.	Qty.	Price	Cost		Date	Emp-loyee	Cost Ctre	Hrs.	Rate	Bonus	Cost		Hrs	OAR	Cost	
				£	p							£	p			£	p
12.6	36807	1	7.18	7	18	11.6	012	A	2	7.00		14	00				
12.6	36808	2	1.24	2	48	12.6	007	A	3.17	6.00		19	02	5.17	3.50	18	10
12.6	36821	1	88.40	88	40												
12.6	36830	1	61.90	61	90												
Total C/F				159	96	Total C/F						33	02	Total C/F		18	10

Expenses						Job Cost Summary	Actual		Estimate	
Date	Ref.	Description	Cost				£	p	£	p
			£	p						
						Direct Materials B/F	159	96	159	96
						Direct Expenses B/F				
						Direct Labour B/F	33	02	90	00
						Direct Cost	192	98		
						Overheads B/F	18	10		
							211	08		
						Admin overhead (add 10%)	21	11		
						= Total Cost	232	19	249	96
						Invoice Price	255	41		
Total C/F						Job Profit/Loss	23	22		

Comments

Job Cost Card Completed by ....

| JOB COST CARD | | | | | | | | | | | | | Job No. | A930 | | |

JOB COST CARD   Job No. A930

| Customer | Mr F Jenkins | Customer's Order No. | Vehicle make | Sierra |

Customer   Mr F Jenkins   Customer's Order No.   Vehicle make   Sierra

Job Description *Overhaul clutch & readjust brakes*   Vehicle reg. no. F109 HEV

Estimate Ref. *2594*   Invoice No.

Quoted price £186.50   Invoice price £194.32   Date to collect 14.6.X3

Material

Date	Req. No.	Qty.	Price	Cost £	Cost p
13.6	36861	1	45.20	45	20
13.6	36874	1	6.95	6	95
13.6	36885	1	8.75	8	75
13.6	36902	2	35.80	71	60
Total C/F				132	50

Labour

Date	Employee	Cost Ctre	Hrs.	Rate	Bonus	Cost £	Cost p
13.6	009	A	2.45	6.50	3.58	19	51
Total C/F						19	51

Overheads

Hrs	OAR	Cost £	Cost p
2.45	3.50	8	58
Total C/F		8	58

Expenses

Date	Ref.	Description	Cost £	Cost p
Total C/F				

Job Cost Summary

	Actual £	Actual p	Estimate £	Estimate p
Direct Materials B/F	132	50	132	50
Direct Expenses B/F				
Direct Labour B/F	19	51	54	00
Direct Cost	152	01		
Overheads B/F	8	58		
Admin overhead (add 10%)	160	59		
	16	06		
= Total Cost	176	65	186	50
Invoice Price	194	32		
Job Profit/Loss	17	67		

Comments

Job Cost Card Completed by ....

JOB COST CARD

		Job No.	B641

Customer	Mr J White	Customer's Order No.	Vehicle make	Peugeot 205 GTE
Job Description	Repair damage to offside front door		Vehicle reg. no.	G 614 SOX
Estimate Ref. 2599		Invoice No.		
Quoted price	£338.68	Invoice price	£355.05	Date to collect	14.6.X3

Material

Date	Req. No.	Qty.	Price	Cost £	Cost p
12.6	36815	1	75.49	75	49
12.6	36816	1	33.19	33	19
12.6	36842	5	6.01	30	05
13.6	36881	5	3.99	19	95

Total C/F: 158 | 68

Labour

Date	Employee	Cost Ctre	Hrs.	Rate	Bonus	Cost £	Cost p
12.6	018	B	1.98	6.50	-	12	87
13.6	018	B	5.92	6.50	-	38	48
					13.65	13	65

Total C/F: 65 | 00

Overheads

Hrs	OAR	Cost £	Cost p
7.9	2.50	19	75

Total C/F: 19 | 75

Expenses

Date	Ref.	Description	Cost £	Cost p
12.6	/	N. Jolley Panel-beating	50	-

Total C/F: 50 | -

Job Cost Summary

	Actual £	Actual p	Estimate £	Estimate p
Direct Materials B/F	158	68	158	68
Direct Expenses B/F	50	00		
Direct Labour B/F	65	00	180	00
Direct Cost	273	68		
Overheads B/F	19	75		
	293	43		
Admin overhead (add 10%)	29	34		
= Total Cost	322	77	338	68
Invoice Price	355	05		
Job Profit/Loss	32	28		

Comments

Job Cost Card Completed by ....

SOLUTION TO PRACTICE DEVOLVED ASSESSMENT 3: STRANGE (PROPERTIES) LTD

Tutorial note. Your approach to this assignment is more important than arriving at an answer that agrees with ours to the penny, so don't be disheartened if your figures are a bit different.

Solution

Task 1

(a)

No.	Date	Description	Code	Total
	November			
1	1	Caretaker - Clerk Court	800/999	76.50
2	1	Sankey Builders, Sheen - Ketley	800/556	600.00
3	1	Post Office	400/001	3.61
4	1	Sundries - Gibbs Ho	800/105	52.80
5	1	Perivale Glass Co.	800/101	317.00
6	3	Motor Mower - Burgess Ct	800/555	263.00
7	4	Electricity - Ketley cl. (to 28.10)	800/556	355.84
8	4	Water rates - Q.C.	800/225	92.00
9	4	Inst. Ch. Surveyors	500/003	515.00
10	5	Hanwell DIY	800/501	69.10
11	8	Law Society (subs)	500/003	742.00
12	8	Inland Revenue	100/003	8,437.50
13	8	Gas - Mallow Cl. (to 5.11)	800/605	81.50
14	9	Cleaners - Seymour M.	800/189	390.01
15	10	Power drill - Laine Ho.	800/501	48.90
16	13	Perivale Roofing	800/101	4,720.00
17	17	Dentons (sols) - re Ashby M.	800/301	723.37
18	17	Coomer PL - Caretaker	800/450	226.00
19	17	Kew Electrics	800/250	590.72
20	17	Southern Electricity (to 15.11)	300/001	1,110.43
21	17	Wyrde St Computer Supplies	400/004	33.00
22	18	Brentford Advertiser	700/001	66.50
23	19	Rentokil - Jones Co.	800/274	856.06
24	21	Neville Ho - Skip Hire (17.10-19.11)	800/376	32.40
25	21	Hanwell Timber	800/501	236.00
26	21	Sankeys - Ketley Clo.	800/556	1,800.00
27	24	Heston Service Station	200/001	8.81
28	24	Bldgs Ins - Oakwood B	800/750	408.00
29	24	Plumbing Supplies (Petersham) Ltd - Kings	800/325	426.80
30	24	Wages - Grasmere Caretaker	800/110	279.19
31	25	BACS - Salaries	100/002	12,187.89
32	25	British Gas - Tilbury	800/890	35.60

No.	Date	Description	Code	Total
	November			
1	26	Hall hire - Wyndham AGM	800/430	32.50
2	26	Sainsbury's	100/010	19.50
3	28	Caretaker - Rodway Ho.	800/001	438.00
4	28	Property Management News	700/001	18.40
5	28	British Telecom	400/002	475.70
6	28	Co. House - Wyndham	800/430	32.00
7	28	Concrete repairs - Tilbury T	800/890	2,250.00
8	28	Acton Skip Hire - 1.11-30.11 - Davison	800/801	32.40
9	28	Brentford Cleaning	300/005	183.00
10	28	Wages - Davison Clo. C/T	800/801	66.10
11	28	Wages - Endymion Pl. C/T	800/675	64.50
12	28	Middlesex Gazette	700/001	22.22
13	28	Ben Smith Stationery Supplies	400/003	178.57
14	28	Electricity - Hennigan Ho. (to 25.11)	800/429	568.35
15	28	Guardian Royal Exchange - Pub. Liab	500/002	970.00
16	28	Guardian Royal Exchange - Richm. Bldgs	800/525	1,630.00
17	28	E Strange Exps	900/001	88.90
18	28	Non-Dom Rates DD	300/003	271.25
19	28	GRE - Jaguar	200/002	1,315.50
20	28	Bank - charges	600/002	70.90
21	28	Bank - interest	600/001	949.93
22				
23				
24				
25				
26				
27				
28				
29				
30				
31				
32				

(b) *Client charges - November 19X2*

		Direct expenses £	Fixed fee £	Share of overheads £	Total £
301	Ashby Mansions	723.37	1,500.00	922.29	3,145.66
555	Burgess Court	263.00	1,500.00	922.29	2,685.29
999	Clerk Court	76.50	1,500.00	922.29	2,498.79
350	Clift Flats	-	1,500.00	922.29	2,422.29
620	Clifton Gardens	-	1,500.00	922.29	2,422.29
450	Coomer Place	226.00	1,500.00	922.29	2,648.29
801	Davison Close	98.50	1,500.00	922.29	2,520.79
261	De Beauvoir Buildings	-	1,500.00	922.29	2,422.29
675	Endymion Place	64.50	1,500.00	922.29	2,486.79
401	Frampton Court	-	1,500.00	922.29	2,422.29
105	Gibbs House	52.80	1,500.00	922.29	2,475.09
101	Glebe Gardens	5,037.00	1,500.00	922.29	7,459.29
110	Grasmere Mansion	279.19	1,500.00	922.29	2,701.48
429	Hennigan House	568.35	1,500.00	922.29	2,990.64
274	Jones Court	856.06	1,500.00	922.29	3,278.35
556	Ketley Close	2,755.84	1,500.00	922.29	5,178.13
325	Kings Buildings	426.80	1,500.00	922.29	2,849.09
501	Laine House	354.00	1,500.00	922.29	2,776.29
250	Loudwater Place	590.72	1,500.00	922.29	3,013.01
100	Matkins Gardens	-	1,500.00	922.29	2,422.29
605	Mallow Close	81.50	1,500.00	922.29	2,503.79
376	Neville House	32.40	1,500.00	922.29	2,454.69
750	Oakwood Buildings	408.00	1,500.00	922.29	2,830.29
225	Queen's Court	92.00	1,500.00	922.29	2,514.29
914	Rhodes Close	-	1,500.00	922.29	2,422.29
001	Rodway House	438.00	1,500.00	922.29	2,860.29
189	Seymour Manor	390.01	1,500.00	922.29	2,812.30
890	Tilbury Tower	2,285.60	1,500.00	922.29	4,707.89
525	Undercliff Gardens	1,630.00	1,500.00	922.29	4,052.29
430	Wyndham Rise	64.50	1,500.00	922.29	2,486.79
		17,794.64	45,000.00	27,668.70	90,463.34

(*Tutorial note.* You should calculate to the penny because clients are invoiced in pounds and pence.)

Task 2

Basis	Legal £	Surveying £	Accounts £	Total £
Employees (W1)	91,264	127,770	54,759	273,793
Floor area (W2)	5,367	10,735	5,367	21,469
Directors (W3)	4,316	4,315	-	8,631
Equal split (W4)	10,313	10,313	10,313	30,939
	111,260	153,133	70,439	334,832

Workings

1   The following expenses should be split on the basis of number of employees.

	£
Wages and salaries	272,255
Staff welfare	1,538
	273,793

	Legal	Surveying	Accounts
Split 5:7:3	£91,264	£127,770	£54,759

(*Tutorial note.* The split should really be done on the basis of the actual payroll analysis. The above is likely to be a reasonable approximation however.)

2   The following expenses can be split on the basis of floor area, which can be seen (by simply looking at the floor plan) to be 1:2:1.

	£
Business rates	3,524
Heat and light	4,775
Buildings depreciation	4,000
Office equipment depreciation	1,752
Repairs and maintenance	834
Cleaning	6,584
	21,469

	Legal	Surveying	Accounts
1:2:1	£5,367	£10,735	£5,367

3   Some of the expenses are incurred solely by the two Strange brothers.

	£
Motor vehicle depreciation	7,500
Subscriptions	1,131
	8,631

These are split 50:50 between the legal and surveying departments.

4   The remaining expenses do not have any obvious basis and it is therefore most appropriate to split these equally between the three departments.

	£
Insurance (see note)	7,600
Telecommunications	1,908
Printing, postage and stationery	3,975
Audit and accountancy	4,500
Bank charges	862
Advertising	1,973
Interest	10,121
	30,939

(*Tutorial note*. It would be better to split the insurance figure between buildings, motor vehicles, public liability, employer's liability and so on, and then apportion it on more appropriate bases, but you have not been given enough information to do this.)

You can now calculate a rate per labour hour, as it were, for the absorption of overheads.

Legal department

$$\frac{£111,260}{1,709} = £65.10 \text{ per hour (say £65)}$$

(Note that the overhead is split over hours spent on existing clients only.)

Surveying department

$$\frac{£153,133}{1,749} = £87.55 \text{ per hour (say £88)}$$

Accounts department

Evenly split over 30 clients:

$$\frac{£70,439}{30} = £2,347.97 \text{ per client per annum (say £2,348)}$$

This allows a schedule to be drawn up as follows.

	Legal		Surveying		Accounts	Total
	Hours	£	Hours	£	£	£
Ashby Mansions	43	2,795	20	1,760	2,348	6,903
Burgess Court	71	4,615	82	7,216	2,348	14,179
Clerk Court	62	4,030	34	2,992	2,348	9,370
Clift Flats	15	975	113	9,944	2,348	13,267
Clifton Gardens	25	1,625	64	5,632	2,348	9,605
Coomer Place	60	3,900	80	7,040	2,348	13,288
Davison Close	49	3,185	52	4,576	2,348	10,109
De Beauvoir Buildings	74	4,810	38	3,344	2,348	10,502
Endymion Place	33	2,145	51	4,488	2,348	8,981
Frampton Court	16	1,040	73	6,424	2,348	9,812
Gibbs House	51	3,315	21	1,848	2,348	7,511
Glebe Gardens	81	5,265	60	5,280	2,348	12,893
Grasmere Mansion	84	5,460	30	2,640	2,348	10,448
Hennigan House	76	4,940	94	8,272	2,348	15,560
Jones Court	61	3,965	66	5,808	2,348	12,121
Ketley Close	49	3,185	36	3,168	2,348	8,701
Kings Buildings	63	4,095	57	5,016	2,348	11,459
Laine House	45	2,925	77	6,776	2,348	12,049
Loudwater Place	73	4,745	48	4,224	2,348	11,317
Matkins Gardens	76	4,940	35	3,080	2,348	10,368
Mallow Close	57	3,705	61	5,368	2,348	11,421
Neville House	24	1,560	92	8,096	2,348	12,004
Oakwood Buildings	117	7,605	40	3,520	2,348	13,473
Queen's Court	51	3,315	18	1,584	2,348	7,247
Rhodes Close	82	5,330	97	8,536	2,348	16,214
Rodway House	64	4,160	88	7,744	2,348	14,252
Seymour Manor	23	1,495	64	5,632	2,348	9,475
Tilbury Tower	29	1,885	59	5,192	2,348	9,425
Undercliff Gardens	80	5,200	71	6,248	2,348	13,796
Wyndham Rise	75	4,875	28	2,464	2,348	9,687
	1,709	111,085	1,749	153,912	70,440	335,437
Total overhead		111,260		153,133	70,439	334,832
(Under-)/over-absorbed		(175)		779	1	605

Notes

1   The (under)/over absorption is due to rounding, for ease of calculation.

2   The amount *actually* charged to each client for the year to 30 September can be estimated as follows, allowing for ex-clients.

$$= \frac{\text{(Administrative expenses + interest)}}{\text{Number of clients}}$$

$$= \frac{£(324,711 + 10,121)}{32.5 \text{(say)}}$$

$$= £10,303$$

Task 3

MEMO

To: Edward Strange
From: John Vernon
Subject: Charges to clients and related matters
Date: 2 December 19X2

CHARGES TO CLIENTS

I refer to your memo of 1 December about charges to clients. I have given this matter some thought and done some calculations. The results are attached. Below I set out my observations and recommendations.

(a)   Part of the problem is due to the way in which we invoice clients. At present our invoices show only a lump sum charge, whereas in fact the charge is made up of three elements, as follows.

    (i)   Expenditure incurred on behalf of the property in question on things like building work, bills for communal electricity, caretaker's wages and so on. The property would have to pay these amounts whether or not we were involved, and they are bound to fluctuate from month to month, just as ordinary household expenses do. For example, for the month just past such expenses range from nil for six clients to £5,037 for Glebe Gardens.

    (ii) Our fixed fee of £1,500 per month charged to all clients.

    (iii) A proportion of our own expenses, divided up equally between clients (see below).

(b)   Point (iii) above is problematic because our own actual expenditure varies from month to month and so, therefore, does the amount charged to clients. For example in November 19X2 we paid a number of bills that we receive on a quarterly basis (like telephone and electricity bills) and some that only occur annually (like your motor insurance premium). However, all of this expenditure will be charged to our clients in one month.

(c)   You may remember that I mentioned to you that I had had some less than complimentary letters from some clients and ex-clients about the fairness of our charges. At present clients for whom we do relatively little work pay the same level of charges as clients for whom we do a great deal of work, and some of them seem to be aware of this and to resent it.

My recommendations are as follows.

(a)   We should show the following separately on our invoices.

    (i)   Amounts paid out on behalf of clients
    (ii) The charge made for our services (the amount on which VAT is calculated)

(b)   Developing (ii), we should charge our clients a standard monthly amount that incorporates the following.

    (i)   Our fixed fee

    (ii) An administration charge based on the amount of work that we expect to do for each client

The calculation of the administration charge will require us to estimate in advance both how much our total administrative expenses will be for the coming year and how much work we expect to do for each client. Pending further discussion, however, I have calculated some figures based on the accounts for the year to 30 September 19X2 and upon your own timesheets for that period and those of your brother.

From the 19X1/X2 accounts we can work out that the amount actually charged to each client to recover administrative expenses and interest paid was about £10,303 for the year. Using the fairer basis that I propose this figure would have ranged from £6,903 for Ashby Mansions to £16,214 for Rhodes Close (neither of these figures includes the fixed fee).

I propose that we adopt the fairer basis, assuming that our costs and expenditure in terms of time can be reasonably accurately forecast. Obviously we need to consider how this change would be presented to clients.

OTHER MATTERS

Since you raised the question I might add that what I am proposing is a form of absorption costing: our costs are being 'absorbed' into the amounts charged to clients on the basis of time spent. A feature of absorption costing is 'under- or over-absorbed overhead', which arises because we use estimates to calculate our absorption rates and an adjustment has to be made once the actual figures are known. For example on the schedules attached you can see the effects of rounding some of the figures to make the calculations easier to do and to understand.

Incidentally, I think you may have been misled about the nature of *process costing*. This is a method of costing that is used mainly in manufacturing businesses where products are made by means of a 'continuous process'. In other words there are always some products that have just been started, some that are completely finished and others that are only partly finished. An organisation like this has to use process costing methods to determine what the cost of their products is at a particular point in time. This is not really appropriate for Strange (Properties) Ltd's business.

SOLUTION TO PRACTICE DEVOLVED ASSESSMENT 4: VALERIE ANDREWS

SECTION 1

Task 1

		£
(a)	8,580 soap packs should have cost ($\times$ £1.20)	10,296
	but did cost (W1)	10,614
	Soap pack price variance	318 (A)

(b)	8,400 rooms should have used	8,400 packs
	but did use	8,580 packs
	Usage variance in packs	180 packs (A)
	$\times$ standard cost per pack	$\times$ £1.20
	Soap pack usage variance in £	£216 (A)

		£
(c)	2,550 hours should have cost ($\times$ £3.60)	9,180
	but did cost (W2)	8,700
	Cleaning labour rate variance	480 (F)

(d)	8,400 rooms should have taken ($\times$ ¼ hr)	2,100 hrs
	but did take	2,550 hrs
	Efficiency variance in hours	450 hrs (A)
	$\times$ standard rate per hour	$\times$ £3.60
	Cleaning labour efficiency variance	£1,620 (A)

Workings

1		£
	6,530 $\times$ £1.20	7,836
	920 $\times$ £1.30	1,196
	1,130 $\times$ £1.40	1,582
		10,614

2		
	1,850 $\times$ £3.00	5,550
	700 $\times$ £4.50	3,150
		8,700

Task 2

The **adverse price variance** could be due to an increase in soap pack prices above the price used in the standard or careless purchasing by the purchasing department.

The **adverse usage variance** may be due to a delivery of low quality soap packs (perhaps packs have items missing or the packaging is ripped) or there may be theft or pilferage of the packs from stores.

The **favourable rate variance** has probably arisen because the proportion of weekday hours worked was greater than anticipated.

The **adverse efficiency variance** may be due to a level of idle time greater than that allowed for in the standard, perhaps because guests had not vacated rooms and cleaners were unable to enter bedrooms.

SECTION 2

Task 1

(a)

	£	
26,500 kg should have cost (× £23)	609,500	
but did cost	662,500	
Material price variance	53,000	(A)

(b)

9,000 units should have used (×3kg)	27,000	kg	
but did use	26,500	kg	
Material usage variance in kg	500	kg	(F)
× standard cost per kg	£23		
Material usage variance in £	£11,500		(F)

(c)

	£	
18,400 hours should have cost (× £23) 20	368,000	
but did cost	349,600	
Labour rate variance	18,400	(F)

(d)

9,000 units should have taken (× 2 hrs)	18,000	hrs	
but did take	18,400	hrs	
Efficiency variance in hours	400	hrs	(A)
× standard rate per hour	£20		
Labour efficiency variance in £	£8,000		(A)

Task 2

STATEMENT OF COST VARIANCES (WEEK 8, QUARTER 4, 1996)

	(F) £	(A) £	£
Material price		53,000	
Material usage	11,500		
Labour rate	18,400		
Labour efficiency		8,000	
Fixed overhead expenditure		300,000	
Fixed overhead capacity		96,000	
Fixed overhead efficiency		24,000	
	29,900	481,000	451,100 (A)

SECTION 3

Task 1

(a)

		£
Budgeted fixed overhead expenditure (12,000 × £67)		804,000
Actual fixed overhead expenditure		824,000
Fixed overhead expenditure variance		20,000 (A)

(b)

		£
Budgeted production at standard rate (12,000 × £67)		804,000
Actual production at standard rate (11,200 × £67)		750,400
Fixed overhead volume variance		53,600 (A)

(c)

Budgeted hours (12,000 × 10)	120,000 hrs
Actual hours	110,000 hrs
Fixed overhead capacity variance in hours	10,000 hrs (A)
× standard rate per hour	× £6.70
Fixed overhead capacity variance	£67,000 (A)

(d)

11,200 units should have taken (× 10 hrs)	112,000 hrs
Actual time taken	110,000 hrs
Fixed overhead efficiency variance in hours	2,000 hrs (F)
× standard rate per hour	× £6.70
Fixed overhead efficiency variance	£13,400 (F)

Task 2

REPORT

To:	Production Director
From:	Assistant Management Accountant
Date:	14 December 1996
Subject:	Performance of Division X - 4 weeks ended 1 December 1996

Set out below is an analysis of the cost variances in Division X for the four-week period ended 1 December 1996.

			£
Variances	(F)	(A)	
	£	£	
Material price		94,000	
Material usage		88,000	
Labour rate		11,000	
Labour efficiency	16,800		
Fixed overhead expenditure		20,000	
Fixed overhead capacity		67,000	
Fixed overhead efficiency	13,400		
	30,200	280,000	249,800 (A)

Task 3

MEMORANDUM

To: Production Director
From: Assistant Management Accountant
Date: 14 December 1996
Subject: Fixed overhead variances

This memorandum provides information on fixed overhead variances. In particular it covers the meaning of the various fixed overhead variances and the ways in which such variances might arise.

The meaning of fixed overhead variances

Whereas labour and material total variances show the effect on costs and hence profit of the difference between what the actual production volume should have cost and what it did cost (in terms of labour or material), if an organisation uses standard absorption costing (as we do), the fixed overhead total variance is the difference between actual fixed overhead expenditure and the fixed overhead absorbed (the under- or over-absorbed overhead).

The total under- or over- absorption is made up of the fixed overhead expenditure variance and the fixed overhead volume variance. The volume variance shows that part of the under- or over-absorbed overhead which is due to any difference between budgeted production volume and actual production volume.

The volume variance can be further broken down into an efficiency variance and a capacity variance. The capacity variance shows how much of the under- or over-absorbed overhead is due to working the labour force or plant more or less than planned whereas the efficiency variance shows the effect of the efficiency of the labour force or plant.

The volume variance and its two subdivisions, the efficiency variance and the capacity variance, measure the extent of under or over absorption due to production volume being different to that planned. Material usage and labour efficiency variances, on the other hand, measure the effect of usage being different from that expected for the actual volume achieved.

Reasons why fixed overhead variances might arise

Under- or over-absorbed fixed overhead is inevitable because the predetermined overhead absorption rates are based on forecasts about expenditure and the level of activity. These forecasts are always likely to be at least a bit inaccurate - the business may forecast both the budgeted expenditure and the volume of activity wrongly.

- Fixed overhead expenditure variance arises when the actual fixed production overhead is different to the budgeted figure. In our case the actual fixed overhead expenditure was £20,000 more than was forecast for the four weeks ended 1 December. This could have arisen, for example, if rent had been increased and this had not been taken account of when making the forecast.

- The fixed overhead volume variance is broken down into efficiency and capacity variances, which have arisen as follows:

The staff worked at a more efficient rate than standard to produce the 11,200 Alphas that were made in the period. They took 2,000 hours less than would have been expected for that level of production, possibly because of increased speed as newer workers became more accustomed to the processes, or less idle time as a result of fewer mechanical breakdowns. This has led to a favourable efficiency variance.

Regardless of the level of efficiency and the number of Alphas produced, the overall total number of hours worked was 10,000 less than budgeted. This could arise through a strike, early closing, or some other incident that led to actual hours worked being less than expected. This created an adverse capacity variance, as fixed overhead was under-absorbed.

SOLUTIONS TO TRIAL RUN
DEVOLVED ASSESSMENT

STANDARD COST CARD

PRODUCT ...... Vegetarian Chilli ......

DESCRIPTION	QUANTITY	COST PER KG/HOUR/ETC	EXTENSION	TOTAL
Materials		£	£	£
Rice	0.125 kg	1.37	0.17	
Lentils	0.0625 kg	0.88	0.06	
Tomatoes	0.167 kg	0.74	0.12	
Mushrooms etc	0.167 kg	1.22	0.20	
Kidney beans	0.167 kg	0.92	0.15	
Chillis	0.025 kg	1.82	0.05	
Cartons	1	0.05	0.05	
SUB-TOTAL				0.80
Labour				
Production	0.025 hr	4.00	0.10	
SUB-TOTAL				0.10
Direct cost				0.90
Variable o/h	0.01 litre	1.75		0.02
Standard variable cost				0.92
Fixed o/h	0.025 hr	10.11		0.25
Standard cost of sale				1.17

STANDARD COST CARD

PRODUCT ....Vegetarian Curry....

DESCRIPTION	QUANTITY	COST PER KG/HOUR/ETC	EXTENSION	TOTAL
Materials		£	£	£
Rice	0.125 kg	1.37	0.17	
Coconut oil	0.167 litre	1.21	0.20	
Spices	0.005 kg	9.66	0.05	
Vegetables	0.167 kg	1.12	0.19	
Cartons	1	0.05	0.05	
SUB-TOTAL				0.66
Labour				
Production	0.033 hr	4.00	0.13	
SUB-TOTAL				0.13
Direct cost				0.79
Variable o/h	0.01 litre	1.75		0.02
Standard variable cost				0.81
Fixed o/h	0.033 hr	8.45		0.28
Standard cost of sale				1.09

(a) (i) Standard quantities are taken from Delia Craddock's letter.

(ii) The standard price per kilogram, hour and so on are calculated as follows, using the price list and compliment slip from Exotic Foods Emporium.

Item	Quantity	Price at 1.3.X3 £	5% £	Mid-year value £	Cost per unit £
Rice	100 kg	130.00	6.50	136.50	1.37
Lentils	100 kg	84.00	4.20	88.20	0.88
Tomatoes	50 kg	35.00	1.75	36.75	0.74
Mushrooms etc	50 kg	58.00	2.90	60.90	1.22
Kidney beans	50 kg	44.00	2.20	46.20	0.92
Chillis	50 kg	86.50	4.33	90.83	1.82
Coconut oil	100 ltrs	115.00	5.75	120.75	1.21
Spices	10 kg	92.00	4.60	96.60	9.66
Vegetables	50 kg	53.50	2.68	56.18	1.12

(iii)   Carton price from quotation.

(b) (i)   Standard times are taken from the business plan.

   (ii)   The standard rates per hour are taken from the offers of employment. The business plan recommended that overtime should not be a regular occurrence. Overtime premium should therefore not be included in the direct cost of the two products.

(c)   Details of the oil are taken from the telephone message. The current price is used as the standard since the message indicates that the price is unlikely to change in the future.

(d) (i)   We need to concern ourselves with the following overheads.

	Annual overhead budget £	
Salary of supervisor	16,000	(from offer of employment)
Salary of storekeeper	12,000	(from offer of employment)
Cleaners (2 hrs × £10 × 5 days × 52 weeks)	5,200	(from contract)
Heat and light	5,000	(from Business Plan)
Overtime (100 hrs × £2.00)	200	(from Business Plan)
	38,400	

Although, in reality, there would be many more overheads such as those associated with the accounting function and so on, we calculate an overhead absorption rate based on the limited information we are given.

		Overhead	Basis of apportionment	Production dept Chilli £	Production dept Curry £	Stores £
(ii)	Directly allocate	Storekeeper's salary				12,000
(iii)	Apportion	Supervisor's salary	Direct labour hours (W1)	7,500	8,500	-
		Cleaners	Area (W2)	2,600	1,560	1,040
		Heat and light	Area (W2)	2,500	1,500	1,000
		Overtime	Hours (W3)	100	100	-
				12,700	11,660	14,040
(iv)	Apportion service dept o'hds		Number of material requisitions (W4)	7,020	7,020	(14,040)
				19,720	18,680	-

Workings

		Chilli	Curry
1	Budgeted production	78,000	66,300
	Time per portion	1.5 mins	2 mins
	Budgeted total time	117,000 mins = 1,950 hrs	132,600 mins = 2,210 hrs
	Proportion of salary	1,950/(1,950 + 2,210)	2,210/(1,950 + 2,210)

2   Chilli department covers $25 \times 50 = 1,250$ m²
   Curry department covers $25 \times 30 = 750$ m²
   Stores covers $25 \times 20 = 500$ m²

   Cleaning costs and heat and light should therefore be shared in the ratio 5:3:2.

3   We are given no indication as to the amount of overtime each product will require. The overhead should therefore be split equally between the two production departments.

4   Ingredients for both products were taken on each of the five occasions items were taken from stores. One simple method of splitting the stores cost is

therefore equally between the two production departments. If Ali and Fred had taken ingredients for just one of the products on one or more occasions then a different apportionment of the overhead would be necessary.

(v) The overhead absorption rate is to be based on direct labour hours according to the business plan. We calculated the budgeted labour hours in each production department in Working 1.

$$\text{Overhead absorption rate - chilli} = \frac{£19,720}{1,950 \text{ hrs}} = £10.11 \text{ per direct labour hour}$$

$$\text{Overhead absorption rate - curry} = \frac{£18,680}{2,210 \text{ hrs}} = £8.45 \text{ per direct labour hour}$$

(e)

5,000 portions should take (× 2 mins)	166.67 hrs
but did take (from clock cards)	170.50 hrs
Efficiency variance, (in hours)	3.83 hrs (A)
× standard rate per hour	× £4
Efficiency variance, (in £)	£15.32 (A)

(f)

STORES LEDGER ACCOUNT

Material: .....Lentils.......................................   Maximum Quantity: ....

Code: ....   Minimum Quantity: ....

Date	Receipts				Issues				Stock		
	G.R.N. No.	Quantity	Unit Price £	Amount £	Stores Req. No.	Quantity	Unit Price £	Amount £	Quantity	Unit Price £	Amount £
1/3		4	84.00	336.00					4	84.00	336.00
1/3						1	84.00	84.00	3	84.00	252.00
8/3						1	84.00	84.00	2	84.00	168.00
15/3						1	84.00	84.00	1	84.00	84.00
22/3						1	84.00	84.00	-		

STORES LEDGER ACCOUNT

Material: ....Vegetables........................ Maximum Quantity: ....

Code: .... Minimum Quantity: ....

Date	Receipts				Issues				Stock		
	G.R.N. No.	Quantity	Unit Price £	Amount £	Stores Req. No.	Quantity	Unit Price £	Amount £	Quantity	Unit Price £	Amount £
1/3		10	53.50	535.00		1	53.50	53.50	10	53.50	535.00
1/3						3	53.50	160.50	9	53.50	481.50
3/3						5	53.50	267.50	6	53.50	321.00
8/3									1	53.50	53.50
12/3		11	53.75	591.25		4	53.73	214.92	12	53.73	644.75
15/3						5	53.73	268.65	8	53.73	429.84
22/3									3	53.73	161.19

(g) Vegetables

These are used in the curry, of which 5,000 portions were made.

5,000 portions should have used (× 0.167 kg)	835 kgs
but did use (drums from stores ledger account × 50 kgs)	900 kgs
Usage variance (in kgs)	65 kgs (A)
× standard cost per kg (from standard cost card)	× £1.12
Usage variance (in £)	£72.80 (A)

(h) During the four-week period the following overheads were absorbed (production volume × OAR per hour × time to produce one portion).

		£
Chilli department:	$5,300 \times £10.11 \times {}^{1.5}/_{60} =$	1,339.58
Curry department:	$5,000 \times £8.45 \times {}^{2}/_{60} =$	1,408.33
		2,747.91

Overheads incurred are as follows.

		£
Supervisor:	$£16,000 \times {}^{1}/_{13}$	1,230.77
Storekeeper:	$£12,000 \times {}^{1}/_{13}$	923.08
Cleaners:	$2 \times £10 \times 5 \times 4$	400.00
Heat and light:	per invoice	629.62
Overtime:	see working	43.50
		3,226.97

Overheads have been under absorbed by £(3,226.97 – 2,747.91) = £479.06

Working

Hours that should have been worked (normal hours) (2 men × 4 weeks × 40 hours)	320.00 hrs
Hours worked (see (b) (171.25 + 170.50))	341.75 hrs
Overtime, in hours	21.75 hrs
× overtime premium per hour	× £2
Overtime, in £	£43.50

Schedule of queries

	Query	*Action*
(a)	Why was the post-lunch entry on Wednesday 17 March handwritten on Fred's clock card?	Speak to supervisor and request he checks that Fred and Ali are adhering to time-keeping procedures.
(b)	How do I allocate the cost of the factory supervisor?	Speak to supervisor
(c)	Labour hours are highly erratic. How does this tie in with stores and supervisor?	Speak to managing director
(d)	Why does the second invoice from Exotic Foods not agree with what was delivered?	Telephone supplier
(e)	Why was the heat and light invoice much greater than anticipated?	Speak to supervisor
(f)	Why did Ali take so much longer than expected to produce the 5,300 portions of chilli?	Speak to supervisor
(g)	Some stocks need reordering	Check that they have been reordered

ORDER FORM

Any books from our AAT range can be ordered by telephoning 0181-740 2211. Alternatively, send this page to our Freepost address or fax it to us on 0181-740 1184, or email us at **publishing@bpp.co.uk**. Or look us up on our Website: http://www.bpp.co.uk

All books are sent out within 48 hours of receipt of your order, subject to availability.

To: BPP Publishing Ltd, Aldine House, Aldine Place, London W12 8AW

Tel: 0181-740 2211   Fax: 0181-740 1184   Email: publishing@bpp.co.uk

Mr / Ms (full name): _____

Day-time delivery address: _____

_____

Postcode: _____   Daytime Tel: (for queries only):_____

Please send me the following quantities of books:

	5/98 Interactive Text	8/98 DA Kit	8/98 CA Kit
FOUNDATION			
Unit 1 Cash Transactions		(5/98)	
Unit 2 Credit Transactions			
Unit 3 Payroll Transactions	(6/98)		
Unit 19 Data Processing (Windows) *	(8/98)		
Unit 21-25 Business Knowledge			

* Contains hands-on tuition and assignments; you will need access to Sage accounting software and BPP data disks

	5/98 Interactive Text	8/98 DA Kit	8/98 CA Kit
INTERMEDIATE			
Unit 4 Financial Records and Accounts		(5/98)	
Unit 5 Cost Information			
Unit 6 Reports and Returns		(5/98)	
Unit 20 Information Technology			
Unit 22: see below			
TECHNICIAN			
Unit 7/8 Core Managing Costs and Allocating Resources			
Unit 9 Core Managing Accounting Systems		(5/98)	
Unit 10 Option Drafting Financial Statements			
Unit 14 Option Cash Management and Credit Control			
Unit 15 Option Evaluating Activities			
Unit 16 Option Implementing Auditing Procedures			
Unit 17 Option Business Taxation Computations	(8/98)	date TBC	
Unit 18 Option Personal Taxation Computations	(8/98)	date TBC	

TOTAL BOOKS [ ] + [ ] + [ ] = [ ]

[ ] @ £9.95 each = £[ ]

Postage and packaging:

UK: £2.00 for each book to maximum of £10

Europe (inc ROI & CD): £4.00 for each book

Rest of the World: £6.00 for each book

P & P   £[ ]

Quantity

Unit 22 Maintaining a Healthy Workplace Interactive Text (postage free)   [ ] @ £3.95   £[ ]

GRAND TOTAL £[ ]

I enclose a cheque for £ _____ (cheques to BPP Publishing Ltd) or charge to Access/Visa/Switch

Card number [ ]

Start date _____   **Expiry date** _____   **Issue no. (Switch only)**____

Signature _____

REVIEW FORM & FREE PRIZE DRAW

All original review forms from the entire BPP range, completed with genuine comments, will be entered into one of two draws on 31 January 1999 and 31 July 1999. The names on the first four forms picked out on each occasion will be sent a cheque for £50.

Name: _____   Address: _____

_____

_____

How have you used this Devolved Assessment Kit?
(Tick one box only)

☐ Home study (book only)

☐ On a course: college _____

☐ With 'correspondence' package

☐ Other _____

Why did you decide to purchase this Devolved Assessment Kit? *(Tick one box only)*

☐ Have used BPP Interactive Texts in the past

☐ Recommendation by friend/colleague

☐ Recommendation by a lecturer at college

☐ Saw advertising

☐ Other _____

During the past six months do you recall seeing/receiving any of the following?
(Tick as many boxes as are relevant)

☐ Our advertisement in *Accounting Technician* magazine

☐ Our advertisement in *Pass*

☐ Our brochure with a letter through the post

Which (if any) aspects of our advertising do you find useful?
(Tick as many boxes as are relevant)

☐ Prices and publication dates of new editions

☐ Information on Interactive Text content

☐ Facility to order books off-the-page

☐ None of the above

Have you used the companion Interactive Text for this subject?   ☐ Yes   ☐ No

Your ratings, comments and suggestions would be appreciated on the following areas

	Very useful	*Useful*	*Not useful*
How to use this Devolved Assessment Kit section	☐	☐	☐
Standards of Competence	☐	☐	☐
Assessment Strategy	☐	☐	☐
Practice Devolved Assessments	☐	☐	☐
Trial Run Devolved Assessments	☐	☐	☐
AAT Sample Simulation	☐	☐	☐
Quality of solutions	☐	☐	☐
Layout of pages	☐	☐	☐
Structure of book and ease of use	☐	☐	☐

	Excellent	*Good*	*Adequate*	*Poor*
Overall opinion of this Kit	☐	☐	☐	☐

Do you intend to continue using BPP Assessment Kits/Interactive Texts? ☐ Yes ☐ No

Please note any further comments and suggestions/errors on the reverse of this page.

Please return to: Clare Donnelly, BPP Publishing Ltd, FREEPOST, London, W12 8BR

REVIEW FORM & FREE PRIZE DRAW (continued)

Please note any further comments and suggestions/errors below

FREE PRIZE DRAW RULES

1   Closing date for 31 January 1999 draw is 31 December 1998. Closing date for 31 July 1999 draw is 30 June 1999.

2   Restricted to entries with UK and Eire addresses only. BPP employees, their families and business associates are excluded.

3   No purchase necessary. Entry forms are available upon request from BPP Publishing. No more than one entry per title, per person. Draw restricted to persons aged 16 and over.

4   Winners will be notified by post and receive their cheques not later than 6 weeks after the relevant draw date. Lists of winners will be published in BPP's *focus* newsletter following the relevant draw.

5   The decision of the promoter in all matters is final and binding. No correspondence will be entered into.